T0352141

PLAYER VS. MONSTER

PLAYFUL THINKING

Jesper Juul, Geoffrey Long, William Uricchio, and Mia Consalvo, editors

The Art of Failure: An Essay on the Pain of Playing Video Games, Jesper Juul, 2013

Uncertainty in Games, Greg Costikyan, 2013

Play Matters, Miguel Sicart, 2014

Works of Game: On the Aesthetics of Games and Art, John Sharp, 2015

How Games Move Us: Emotion by Design, Katherine Isbister, 2016

Playing Smart: On Games, Intelligence, and Artificial Intelligence, Julian Togelius, 2018

Fun, Taste, & Games: An Aesthetics of the Idle, Unproductive, and Otherwise Playful, John Sharp and David Thomas, 2019

Real Games: What's Legitimate and What's Not in Contemporary Video Games, Mia Consalvo and Christopher A. Paul, 2019

Achievement Relocked: Loss Aversion and Game Design, Geoffrey Engelstein, 2020

Play Like a Feminist, Shira Chess, 2020

Ambient Play, Larissa Hjorth and Ingrid Richardson, 2020

Making Games: The Politics and Poetics of Game Creation Tools, Stefan Werning, 2021

Treacherous Play, Marcus Carter, 2022

Repairing Play: A Black Phenomenology, Aaron Trammell, 2023

Player vs. Monster: The Making and Breaking of Video Game Monstrosity, Jaroslav Švelch, 2023

PLAYER VS. MONSTER

THE MAKING AND BREAKING
OF VIDEO GAME MONSTROSITY

JAROSLAV ŠVELCH

The MIT Press
Cambridge, Massachusetts
London, England

The MIT Press would like to thank the anonymous peer reviewers who provided comments on drafts of this book. The generous work of academic experts is essential for establishing the authority and quality of our publications. We acknowledge with gratitude the contributions of these otherwise uncredited readers.

This book was set in Stone Serif and URW DIN by Westchester Publishing Services. Printed and bound in the United States of America.

Library of Congress Cataloging-in-Publication Data

Names: Švelch, Jaroslav, author.
Title: Player vs. monster : the making and breaking of video game monstrosity / Jaroslav Švelch.
Other titles: Player versus monster
Description: Cambridge, Massachusetts : The MIT Press, [2023] | Series: Playful thinking | Includes bibliographical references and index.
Identifiers: LCCN 2022013927 (print) | LCCN 2022013928 (ebook) | ISBN 9780262047753 (hardcover) | ISBN 9780262373234 (epub) | ISBN 9780262373241 (pdf)
Subjects: LCSH: Monsters in video games.
Classification: LCC GV1469.34.M66 S84 2023 (print) | LCC GV1469.34.M66 (ebook) | DDC 794.8/47—dc23/eng/20221006
LC record available at https://lccn.loc.gov/2022013927
LC ebook record available at https://lccn.loc.gov/2022013928

10 9 8 7 6 5 4 3 2 1

To Iggy, who is absolutely not a monster

CONTENTS

ON THINKING PLAYFULLY

Many people (we series editors included) find video games exhilarating, but it can be just as interesting to ponder why that is so. What do video games do? What can they be used for? How do they work? How do they relate to the rest of the world? Why is play both so important and so powerful?

Playful Thinking is a series of short, readable, and argumentative books that share some playfulness and excitement with the games that they are about. Each book in the series is small enough to fit in a backpack or coat pocket, and combines depth with readability for any reader interested in playing more thoughtfully or thinking more playfully. This includes, but is by no means limited to, academics, game makers, and curious players.

So, we are casting our net wide. Each book in our series provides a blend of new insights and interesting arguments with overviews of knowledge from game studies and other areas. You will see this reflected not just in the range of titles in our series, but in the range of authors creating them. Our basic assumption is simple: video games are such a flourishing medium that any new perspective on them is likely to show us something unseen or forgotten, including those from such unconventional voices as artists, philosophers, or specialists in other industries or fields of study. These books are bridge builders, cross-pollinating both areas with new knowledge and new ways of thinking.

At its heart, this is what Playful Thinking is all about: new ways of thinking about games and new ways of using games to think about the rest of the world.

Jesper Juul
Geoffrey Long
William Uricchio
Mia Consalvo

ACKNOWLEDGMENTS

When I was a teenager, my gaming buddies and I would call them "potvory," one of the many Czech synonyms for "monsters." There were so many, and they were so fascinating: from the killer toilets of *Manic Miner* to the slimes and mummies of *Dungeon Master* and the *Wizardry* series. More than fifteen years later, as a doctoral student at Charles University in Prague, I was still just as intrigued by monsters— only this time they were the repulsive necromorphs of *Dead Space* or the corrupted angels of *Bayonetta*. The first time I realized they could be worthwhile subjects of research was in 2011, when I noticed a call for chapters for a book called *Monster Culture in the 21st Century: A Reader*, edited by Marina Levina and Diem-My Bui. The editors liked my idea of writing about video game monsters and gave me excellent, hands-on feedback on my chapter that made me realize how intellectually complex the topic really was—and that it deserved a book of its own.

The idea lay dormant while I was working on *Gaming the Iron Curtain*, a book about the history of games in 1980s Czechoslovakia. I returned to monsters in 2017, when I started a two-year postdoc within the Games and Transgressive

Aesthetics research project at the University of Bergen, funded by the Research Council of Norway and headed by Kristine Jørgensen. I am very grateful for this opportunity to study monsters full-time, and I would like to thank Kristine as well as Kristian Bjørkelo, Ea Christina Willumsen, Rune Klevjer, and Torill Mortensen for being such kind and inspiring colleagues. During my postdoc, I co-organized several workshops and panels on video games and monstrosity. My thanks go to all the participants for their contributions and feedback, especially to Daniel Vella and Sarah Stang, who co-organized them with me. Chapters 1 and 2 were drafted in Bergen and include ideas and arguments first presented at the 2018 Philosophy of Computer Games conference in Copenhagen in a paper called "Encoding Monsters: 'Ontology of the Enemy' and Containment of the Unknown in Role-Playing Games." I completed the manuscript in Prague with support from Charles University's PRIMUS grant program, project no. 21/HUM/005.

Besides those already mentioned, many other people have helped me along the way. Clara Fernández-Vara and Matthew Weise have shared with me many monster-related examples and observations over the years. Their knowledge of video game monsters far surpasses mine, and I have only written this book because they had not. My brother Jan Švelch has, as always, read all my drafts and offered instant and honest feedback; he also contributed his findings about the production side of video game monsters to chapter 3. On top of their other contributions, Kristine Jørgensen and Daniel Vella provided detailed and thoughtful feedback on the whole manuscript. (I am nevertheless the only person responsible for all the remaining bugs.) Charlotte Bruckermann, Marisa Morán

Jahn, and Henry Jenkins gave me crucial reading tips and inspiring advice; Aaron Trammell and Rachael Hutchinson shared with me some of their vast knowledge of *D&D* and Japanese popular culture, respectively. Abhimanyu Das proofread my drafts and polished my prose, often on a very short notice. The staff at the Strong Museum of Play kindly and enthusiastically assisted me in finding monsters in their libraries and collections. Luis Blackaller created the marvelous cover from the ground up while listening to my fanciful ideas. I would also like to thank Tereza Fousek Krobová for helping me organize monster-themed focus groups and the focus group participants themselves.

I am grateful to the MIT Press editors who have worked with me on this project—Noah Springer and Doug Sery—as well as the series editors—Mia Consalvo, Jesper Juul, Geoffrey Long, and William Uricchio—for putting their faith in this book and helping it see the light of day. In addition, I would like to thank the three anonymous reviewers for useful comments and pointers.

Outside of the academic world, my wife Lenka Švelchová, our son Ignác, and our dog Lojzička gave me all the support I needed to finish this book. Without them, I would be lost in the dungeons.

Finally, I would like to acknowledge all the monsters I had to kill during the making of this book. I am sorry, monsters, but I had no choice. Or did I?

INTRODUCTION

A dungeon without monsters would be dull stuff.[1]
—From the 1975 manual of *Tunnels & Trolls*, an early
tabletop role-playing game

Seattle's Living Computers Museum is one of the few places
in the world where one can run a PLATO (Programmed Logic
for Automated Teaching Operations) terminal, and I have
come here to meet some of video gaming's earliest monsters.
The pioneering PLATO system was designed in the 1960s for
the purposes of education, but today it is fondly remembered
for hosting some of the first computer role-playing games
(RPGs).[2] I sit down in front of a portrait-oriented monitor and
a sturdy, wood-and-metal keyboard, log in, and run a version
of *dnd*, an early adaptation of the *Dungeons & Dragons* tabletop RPG.[3] The intro screen instructs me to wait while the program is "Loading monsters." (A later version says: "Wait while
monsters breed.") Finally, my player character—a helmeted
knight—appears in a dungeon. After a bit of exploration, I
encounter a Level 1 demon (see figure 0.1). Like everything
else on the screen, the demon is rendered in monochrome

FIGURE 0.1

The protagonist of *dnd* version 5.4 (1977) encountering a demon on the PLATO terminal at the Living Computers Museum in Seattle. (Photo by author.)

orange, glowing brightly against the black background. With its small, smug mouth and three-pronged pitchfork, it stands cute but resolute. The demon and my knight take turns fighting; I fail and I die. I try again. I fail, I win, I fail. In due time, I meet other grotesque monsters: a Balrog, a wombat, a spectre, a vampire, each drawn with a level of detail disproportionate to the simple lines that make up the environment.

Though hailing from the mid-1970s, these creatures fulfil the same roles as many of the monsters in today's video games. They keep up the flow of gameplay by offering adequate doses of challenge. They are an attraction, showcasing the artistry of the creators and the graphical possibilities of the machine. They appear in order to kill me—or to be killed—and then disappear again, flickers of automated agency in a rudimentary game world. In this book, I want to give the spotlight to such creatures, ranging from the pixelated aliens of *Space Invaders* to the high-definition Trolls of the recent *God of War* reboot.[4] My aim is to show how monsters invaded video games and how video games have, in turn, affected our notions of monstrosity and otherness.

Monster is a word loaded with meaning. In addition to fantastic beasts and scary creatures like vampires or zombies, it used to refer to "monstrous births" and to humans whose physiognomy was considered abnormal. As such, the word has been abused to oppress and exclude groups of people who do not conform to normative definitions of humanity.[5] In metaphorical usage, it can denote immoral, despicable humans like tyrants, mass murderers, or terrorists. And, if we stretch it even further, it may refer to just about anything unusually large or otherwise out of the norm. We can also, like posthumanist and feminist writers and scholars, use the word in a hopeful and positive way, to describe entities, processes, or methods that resist the current norms of categorization and the powers that be.[6]

A book this short cannot account for all shades of monstrosity. I start from a more restrictive, traditionalist definition. Like the film scholar and horror theorist Noël Carroll, I limit the scope of my monster research to "any being not believed to exist now according to contemporary science."[7] While some of my findings may also apply to humans, living beasts, or robots, my primary focus is on nonhuman fantastic beings, from the alien to the zombie. Many of these creatures are familiar, as video games have borrowed them from film, comics, literature, folklore, and myth; their audiovisual representation and narrative grounding can thus be analyzed through existing literature on monsters in other media. There is, however, one important difference: most of the time, games do not merely have us observe the struggle against monsters, but instead stage a direct—albeit simulated—conflict between the player and the monster. As in the aforementioned *dnd* example, monsters become targets of player action—dynamic obstacles that can be surmounted by perseverance, wits, or hand-eye coordination. The discussion in this book revolves around this very conflict, offering an approach to monstrosity that is medium specific and mindful of the computational and rule-based nature of video games.

Despite their central role in gaming, the game studies discipline has paid monsters very little attention. Existing scholarship tends to focus on narrow categories of creatures, most often zombies. Such specialized scholarship includes work by Matthew Weise, Diane Carr, and Hans-Joachim Backe with Espen Aarseth, as well as a recent volume edited by Stephen J. Webley and Peter Zackariasson entitled *The Playful Undead and Video Games*.[8] Literature exploring related genres and themes, such as Bernard Perron's work on horror games and several texts in Tanya Krzywinska's oeuvre on Gothic aesthetics in gaming, also touches upon monsters.[9] Carly Kocurek's analysis of "alternative blood" in violent games provides a valuable discussion of the dehumanization of video game enemies.[10] Sarah Stang and Bo Ruberg have applied gender studies and queer theory perspectives to explore monstrous representations in video games.[11] There has been, however, limited insight into video game monsters as a general conceptual category, or into their specific roles and functions within the medium.

In this book, I argue that these creatures embody a specific kind of computational and commodified otherness that is designed to be confronted and defeated—it is the great paradox of video game monsters that they seem dangerous but are, by and large, designed to be beaten. In addition to analyzing the status quo of monster design, I also gauge the potential of the medium to present more nuanced and complex forms of monstrosity. My approach combines media history and game analysis with an examination of behind-the-scenes processes of game development inspired by the growing field of game production studies.[12]

Like any rigorous investigation of monsters, this book is interdisciplinary in nature. While the terms *monster theory* and *teratology* are sometimes used to label work on monstrosity, such work invariably draws from the lineage of various branches of the humanities, including philosophy, cultural history, art history, anthropology, archaeology, literary theory, media studies, film studies, gender studies, and folkloristics. One of my ambitions is to combine these disparate perspectives to shed light on the monsters of video games. Moreover, I believe that the figure of the monster is a fitting lens for exploring and questioning some of the core design conventions of the video game medium.

Along with a selection of historical and contemporary games, this book draws from paratextual sources such as art books, developer testimonies, and design documents. Many of my examples, especially in the first two chapters, come from 1970s and 1980s tabletop and video games. In addition to their importance in the historical narrative, these games provide important clues for understanding how thinking about monsters in games had formed; before monster combat became one of the default types of video game action, some game creators felt the need to spell out what we now accept as a given: explicitly describing the role of monsters in their games. Although the player's perspective is not explicitly covered in this book, my thinking on the topic is also informed by my concurrent research on player reception of video game monsters, building on online discussion analysis and focus group interviews with expert players.[13]

The book is divided into four chapters. Chapter 1 introduces the basic tenets of monster scholarship and invokes them to discuss the tension between two distinct ways of representing monsters—*sublime* and *contained* monstrosity. In its latter half, the chapter traces the social and cultural developments that shaped video games' approach to monstrosity—the consumerist monster culture, the Cold War–era cybernetics, and the introduction of computational servants, sometimes called *daemons*.

Chapter 2 revisits the time when monsters gained their status of go-to video game antagonists. It argues that monsters only rarely appeared in games before the introduction of the *player vs. environment* mode of play in the 1970s and investigates two titles that contributed to the proliferation of monsters: the *Dungeons & Dragons* tabletop RPG and the arcade hit *Space Invaders*. The chapter concludes with a summary and critique of the player vs. environment formula, highlighting its anthropocentrism and its questionable equation of otherness with enmity.

Chapter 3 ventures behind the scenes of monster design and opens with a summary of historical approaches to the craft of creating monsters, ranging from ancient and medieval art to stop-motion monster film. Using examples of mainstream, big-budget titles like the 2018 reboot of *God of War*, the bulk of the chapter shows how the creative work of monster design is shaped by the player vs. environment mode of gameplay, by the representational conventions of figurative art, and by the affordances of digital technology. It also discusses boss monsters as a pinnacle of monster design.

Chapter 4 explores games that *subvert* the player vs. environment model by questioning the heroism of the monster killer and the monsters' otherness, or by unleashing enemies that cannot be engaged with in conventional video game combat. It argues that to design monsters that are in sync with contemporary understanding of otherness and the current societal threats, video games should question the simplistic and anthropocentric notion of fictional creatures as expendable and calculable enemies.

1

TAMING THE MONSTER

Monsters cannot be announced. One cannot say: "Here are our monsters," without immediately turning the monsters into pets.[1]

—Jacques Derrida

During my playthrough of *Bloodborne*, a 2015 action RPG praised for its monster design, I entered a darkened and spacious cave that felt like a boss arena—a part of the game world where my character would fight one of her many battles with special "boss" monsters.[2] I kept my guard up, but nobody attacked me. I ran forward, only to find a huge monster curled up and sleeping. Basking in moonlight, it looked quite otherworldly, with coral-like tentacles fluttering around its head and giant wings with a floral texture. Up to this point, I had met hundreds of monsters and killed them all. I had learned how to dispose of them efficiently—and looked up their weak spots online if I was struggling too much. But now, I hesitated. This creature looked too wonderful and, at the same time, too powerful. I ended up watching it for a couple of minutes before leaving the cave. I did not take a screenshot and I did not even see the creature's name, because *Blood-borne* only displays the name of the boss when you enter combat; only later did I discover that its name was Ebrietas, Daughter of the Cosmos. This nonbattle turned out to be a powerful experience, but its power stemmed mostly from the contrast between this and my other monster encounters. To me, it represented the paradox common to many monster narratives, both in video games and in other media. There is a mysterious monster we are supposed to fear and a hero who—using strength, skill, and wits—defeats that monster. But if we know that the monster can be defeated, can it still be fearsome? If we know its name and its weak spots, is it still mysterious? This paradox results from the tension between *sublime* and *contained* monstrosity.

This chapter will explain this tension based on the growing body of monster scholarship, laying the theoretical foundation for the chapters that follow. After introducing the concepts of sublime and contained monstrosity, it will discuss how monsters are turned into enemies or playthings, and therefore objectified. The second half of the chapter will show how various approaches to monstrosity have played out in recent history, chronicling the invasion of monsters into popular culture and the impact of cybernetics and Cold War–era military paradigms on enemy representation. Finally, it will show how video game monsters are related to *bugs* and *daemons* that embody the agency of computer technology.

SUBLIME MONSTROSITY

Monsters—at least those discussed in this book—do not exist in a strictly physical sense, but they do perform real cultural work. The original Latin word *monstrum* means "that which reveals" or "that which warns." As the monster scholar Jeffrey Jerome Cohen puts it, "the monster signifies something other than itself," and is "a construct and a projection."[3] Monsters speak to our deeper fears and voice the anxieties of our cultures and societies. To convey its message, a monster must grip our attention and then emotionally and cognitively affect us. Many scholars observe that monsters fill us with awe and terror. The philosopher Stephen Asma calls this line of thinking the "sublime thesis," based on Immanuel Kant's understanding of the sublime.[4] In Kant's words, an object that evokes the sublime does so because it appears "to be ill-adapted to our faculty of presentation, and to do violence, as it were, to the imagination."[5] In other words, the sublime is an experience of something that overwhelms our cognitive and intellectual abilities, whether it is unfathomably beautiful or incomprehensibly monstrous.[6] Kant further distinguishes between the *mathematical* sublime, evoked by that which is "immeasurable and colossal" and makes us think of infinitude, and the *dynamic* sublime, caused by the sight of the "devastating superior forces of nature."[7]

The sublime thesis goes hand in hand with the observation that monsters breach boundaries. They can do so in several ways. First, we can think of monsters as mysterious invaders from beyond the known world—harbingers of cosmic chaos. The religion scholar Timothy Beal sees them as "threatening figures of anomaly within the well-established and accepted order of things, [representing] the outside that has gotten inside."[8] He gives the example of the sea monster Leviathan in the Old Testament. While some psalms describe it as God's creation, others paint it as a dreadful chaos monster that is *beyond* God's authority, "menacing both the order of creation and its creator God."[9]

Second, following Julia Kristeva's theory of *abjection*, we can understand the monster as an "abject" complement to the human subject. Drawing from psychoanalysis, Kristeva suggests that horror arises when we are confronted with suppressed parts of ourselves, both physical and psychological. Abject monstrosity thus consists of the things we would rather keep inside—the skeleton and the bodily fluids, as well as our hidden fears and desires. In Kristeva's view, the abject is "what disturbs identity, system, order. What does not respect borders, positions, rules. The in-between, the ambiguous, the composite."[10] As it remains, in essence, a part of us, the monstrous resists becoming an object of human action. According to Kristeva, "it is not an ob-ject facing me, which I name or imagine."[11]

Finally, according to Noël Carroll's formalist theory of horror, monsters are *cognitively* disorienting because they transgress category boundaries. Monsters fit "neither the conceptual scheme of the characters nor, more importantly, the reader,"[12] because they are categorically interstitial, categorically contradictory, incomplete, or formless.[13] In other words, sublime horror does not rely solely on screams, gore, and jump scares—it also confounds our cognitive faculties. Carroll distinguishes between two types of category jamming: *fusion* and *fission*. While fusion "hinges upon conflating, combining, or condensing distinct and/or opposed categorical elements in a spatio-temporally continuous monster," fission distributes these elements onto spatially or temporally separate but metaphysically related beings.[14] An undead zombie is a fusion, as it is at once an animate being and a human corpse, while a werewolf is a fission, as it is sometimes human, sometimes animal.

In all its theoretical articulations, sublime monstrosity should be understood as a normative yardstick of monster representation rather than a feature common to all fictional monsters. After all, the monsters of contemporary popular culture rarely attain the perplexing qualities formulated by the sublime thesis. Ancient myths do, however, contain examples of sublime monstrosity, such as the monster god Marduk from the Mesopotamian epic of creation:

> His limbs were ingeniously made beyond comprehension,
> Impossible to understand, too difficult to perceive.
> Four were his eyes, four were his ears;
> When his lips moved, fire blazed forth.
> The four ears were enormous
> And likewise the eyes; they perceived everything.
> Highest among the gods, his form was outstanding.
> His limbs were very long, his height outstanding.[15]

Marduk, or at least this version of him, is an outsize figure who wields a tempest, a tornado, and a whirlwind as weapons and whose individual features are left to our imagination.[16] So are those of Grendel from the Old English epic poem *Beowulf*, who eludes overt description and measurement, although we do learn, for example, that he can seize thirty men at once.[17] In twentieth-century horror fiction, sublime horror was famously embraced by H. P. Lovecraft, who held the opinion that "the oldest and strongest kind of fear is fear of the unknown" and made lack of description his trademark stylistic device.[18] In the following excerpt from the short story "The Outsider," the monstrous narrator describes what he sees in the mirror:

> I cannot even hint what it was like, for it was a compound of all that is unclean, uncanny, unwelcome, abnormal, and detestable. It was the ghoulish shade of decay, antiquity, and desolation; the putrid, dripping eidolon of

unwholesome revelation; the awful baring of that which
the merciful earth should always hide. God knows it was
not of this world—or no longer of this world—yet to my
horror I saw in its eaten away and bone-revealing outlines
a leering, abhorrent travesty on the human shape; and in
its mouldy, disintegrating apparel an unspeakable quality
that chilled me even more.[19]

This redundant but potent barrage of adjectives dances
around the monster without committing to explicit description, demonstrating Lovecraft's thesis that true cosmic horror
is unspeakable. In his stories, humanity teeters on the brink of
destruction by forces far beyond our imagination. This quality,
however, makes his writing notoriously difficult to adequately
adapt into video games, in which—as we will see—monsters
tend to be visualized and simulated.[20]

CONTAINED MONSTROSITY

Alongside the ideal of sublime monstrosity, there has long been
a parallel tendency to represent monsters as *contained*, or sub-
sumed into the structures of human knowledge and agency.
This tendency stems from the more general urge to control the
unknown. In the history of medieval Europe, and also China,
collecting monsters into compendia went hand in hand with
the mapping of unknown territories. Pliny the Elder's *Natural History* (compiled around 79 AD) and medieval bestiaries
enumerated and described monsters from far corners of the
world, many of them originating as misinterpretations or exag-
gerations of existing animals (see figure 1.1). Medievalists such
as Asa Mittman have shown that maps and bestiaries reflect
the process of containment through which a culture defines

FIGURE 1.1

A dragon strangling an elephant in the Aberdeen Bestiary from twelfth-century England. (Folio 65v, reprinted with permission from University of Aberdeen.)

its borders and distinguishes itself from monstrous others.[21] Reading the description of the Great Dragon from a standard twelfth-century European bestiary, situated in the section on serpents, we learn that "he is born in Ethiopia and India, where the heat is continually sultry."[22] The volumes contained scary monsters but also sought to comfort the reader by suggesting that, as the scholar of Chinese bestiaries Richard Strassberg puts it, "all the important objects of reality had been collected and ordered according to a fundamental taxonomy and that these things were now manageable and available for exploitation."[23] The same can be said about Japanese Edo-period monster compendia such as 1737's *Picture Scroll of a Hundred Monsters*, or early modern grimoires of Christian demonology, which partitioned evil into a chart of hierarchically organized entities.[24] Such databases of monstrosity are, in a way, ready to become games. In his discussion of Dante's *Inferno*, Eugene Thacker notes that its rendering of Hell is carefully, quasi-scientifically stratified into a series of levels, "as if Dante had, unwittingly, designed Hell as a video game."[25] Indeed, in 2010 *Dante's Inferno* was released for the consoles.[26]

The sublime thesis assumes that information about a monster is missing, obscure, or incomprehensible. The amount and the quality of information is, to some extent, medium specific. Illustrations, plastic toys, or 3D models in video games may impart more information than would be gleaned from verbal description. As Margrit Shildrick notes of monstrous imagery, "there is always a certain closure in the static image which transfixes and holds in place that which might otherwise remain unknown."[27] A fitting example is that of the *tupilaq*, a fearsome monster of the Inuit religion of Greenland. Created by a shaman to kill an adversary, the tupilaq was assembled from body parts of dead animals or even dead children, combined with objects belonging to the victim, and brought to life by ritualistic chants.[28] Although people generally agreed on the existence and basic characteristics of the tupilaq, its image was always temporary, and visual descriptions varied from person to person. However, as Europeans started to colonize Greenland in the late nineteenth century, they were curious to see a depiction of this monster, and the Inuit people started to carve grotesque, whale-bone statuettes to satisfy the demand.[29] As the tupilaq was turned into a tangible commodity, its sublime monstrosity was contained, leaving it as an attractive but powerless object. For the same reason, the old Babylonian drawings of Marduk might seem underwhelming from today's perspective (see figure 1.2). Despite being a monster god, he was submitted to the contemporary conventions of figurative art and depicted as merely a bearded man wearing a star-adorned tunic.

The containment of sublime monstrosity echoes the general tendency in art and culture to appropriate and bowdlerize transgressive content, described by Torill Mortensen and Kristine Jørgensen as the *paradox of transgression*:

> When transgressive practices are integrated into culture, either through the carnival, a rite of passage, transgressive art in an art gallery, or transgressive media expressions hailed for their edginess, these practices are accepted into a particular cultural context in which they are rarely experienced as profoundly transgressive.[30]

In other words, what was once a scary, transgressive monster gradually becomes part of our everyday cultural milieu and loses its edge. Containment of monstrosity is, however, not

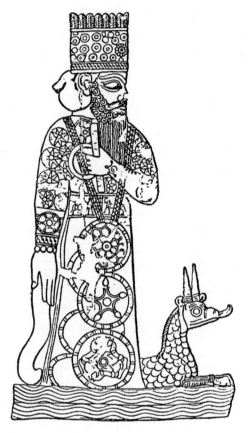

FIGURE 1.2
Stone relief image of the Babylonian monster god Marduk. (Wellcome Library, London. Reprinted under Creative Commons BY 4.0 license.)

a one-way street. As Cohen reminds us, the monster "always rises from the dissection table as its secrets are about to be revealed and vanishes into the night."[31] When one generation's monsters become the next one's playthings, new monsters can arise, and the old ones can receive new meanings. As shown by Roger Luckhurst, the zombie, for example, has gone through several cycles of reinvention. In nineteenth-century Haiti, the zombie (or, in its older spelling, *zombi*) signified the oppression and dehumanization of slavery and forced labor. Early zombie films such as *White Zombie*, in contrast, staged a confrontation between white, Western heroes and the sinister Caribbean others—voodoo masters and their zombie guardians. George Romero's zombies evoked the horrors of the Vietnam War in 1968's *Night of the Living Dead* and the anxieties of consumerism in 1978's *Dawn of the Dead*. And finally, the "fast" zombies of films like *28 Days Later* foregrounded the fear of contagion through biological warfare in an increasingly globalized world.[32] Along with the shifting context and narratives, the behaviors of these creatures also changed, from small groups of undead servants to the unstoppable hordes of the zombie apocalypse.

The sublime versus contained dichotomy should therefore be understood not as a binary but as a scale. Video games have often relied on "edgy," transgressive aesthetics and monstrous imagery to shock and disgust the player. Battles with boss monsters especially attempt to fill the player with fear and awe. But as this book will try to show, the medium leans largely toward contained monstrosity.

THE ENEMY AND THE PLAYTHING

Naming, describing, and visualizing the monster amounts to capturing and making it into an object of human action. This objectification can have two major outcomes: the monster is presented as an *enemy* or a *plaything*. The former is a cornerstone of many mythical and folkloric narratives: a typical hero's journey involves slaying or outsmarting the monstrous enemy, who either threatens the hero's community or resides in a dangerous foreign territory.[33] There is a dark side to this virtuous quest. Embodying the fear of the other, monstrous representations have been deployed in service of racism, sexism, and prejudice in general. Calling someone or something a monster makes them vulnerable to oppression, violence, and extinction.

In Europe in the late Middle Ages, there was a very thin boundary between representations of fantastic monstrous races, such as dog-headed people, and Muslims, who were scornfully described as "a race of dogs." Art historian Debra Higgs Strickland argues that the constructed stereotypes of Jews, Muslims, Black Africans, and Mongols were just as imaginary as fantastic races and were considered "physically aberrant, culturally abhorrent, and, most importantly, ignorant of God." All these groups then suffered grave consequences for their perceived monstrosity, ranging from social subordination and enslavement to expulsion and murder.[34] The convergence between monstrous representations and racial stereotypes works both ways: while othered people are shown as monstrous, fictional monsters take on stereotypical features of racial others, further perpetuating the stereotypes. The monster of Mary Shelley's *Frankenstein*, for instance, bears many similarities to nineteenth-century depictions of Black Africans, whose presumed features included abnormal strength and speed as well as cruelty and vengefulness.[35] And, in the end, Lovecraft's "cosmic" horror cannot be separated from his own xenophobic fear of anyone not Anglo-Saxon.[36]

Monstrous representations of femininity and motherhood have been deconstructed in the work of Barbara Creed. Following Kristeva's psychoanalytical approach to abjection, Creed relates the monstrous-feminine to the fear of castration. In her view, patriarchal discourses tend to represent femininity as a danger that needs to be contained, embodying it in monsters such as the Gorgons, sirens, monstrous mothers, or, most famously, witches.[37] Just as Medusa was slain by Perseus, monstrous women of myth and fiction tend to be eliminated by a male subject.[38]

A second, less confrontational form of monster objectification is its reduction to a toy or a *plaything*. Medieval bestiaries tended to be used as educational material—not to teach about monsters, but to teach Latin or Christian ethics. The dragon was not there to intimidate but to illustrate, amuse, and entertain.[39] The same can be said about dragon-kites. Although originally used for military purposes—to inspire troops and terrify the enemy—flying them later became a playful, recreational activity.[40] Yet when a monster becomes a plaything, it inevitably loses some of its sublime qualities. In his influential book on play and games, Roger Caillois points out that play generally dispels mystery. Like his predecessor Johan Huizinga, he contends that play is separate from quotidian life and that rules of play are often derived from sacred rituals.[41] But while play often uses mystery as a premise, its nature is "nearly always spectacular or ostentatious":

> Without doubt, secrecy, mystery, and even travesty can be transformed into play activity, but it must be immediately pointed out that this transformation is necessarily to the detriment of the secret and mysterious, which play exposes, publishes, and somehow *expends*. In a word, play tends to remove the very nature of the mysterious.[42]

Mortensen and Jørgensen similarly note that "when transgressions take place in a playful context, they change as they become play elements. Even in situations when their representation remains abject and repulsive, they are play-things."[43] The process of turning a monster into a plaything is wonderfully captured in the 1981 British computer game *3D Monster Maze*, in which the protagonist must escape the titular maze while evading a gigantic Tyrannosaurus Rex (see figure 1.3). The events of gameplay itself are framed as a visit to a circus. In the introductory sequence, a figure of a circus barker exclaims:

> Roll up, roll up, see the amazing Tyrannosaurus Rex, King of the Dinosaurs, in his lair. Perfectly preserved in silicon since prehistoric times, he is brought to you for your entertainment and exhilaration. If you dare to enter his lair, you do so at your own risk. The management

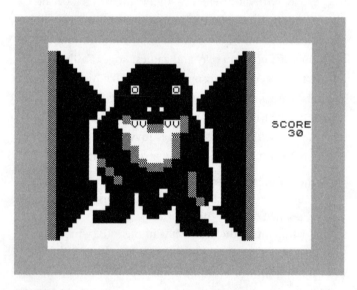

FIGURE 1.3
The Tyrannosaurus Rex in *3D Monster Maze* (1981).

accept no responsibility for the health and safety of the adventurer who enters his realm.[44]

The monologue hints at the reptile's sublime qualities by calling him the King of the Dinosaurs and referring to his prehistoric origin. At the same time, he is preserved (contained) in silicon (meaning the computer's circuitry), presumably by the game's programmers. The circus framing highlights the playful and controlled nature of the encounter while spelling out the game's connection to existing manifestations of monster culture, such as dinosaur parks. The monster is portrayed as dangerous to the health and safety of the "adventurer," but the player is supposed to be entertained, as the play situation insulates them from physical danger.

MONSTERS FOR SALE

Monstrous representations abound in today's popular cultures, packaged as amusements, attractions, and toys for popular consumption. Although this trend may have already started with medieval bestiaries, twentieth-century entertainment and toy industries proved remarkably efficient in flooding the market with monsters of all kinds. Monsters had already appeared in German silent films of the 1910s and '20s and in 1930s Hollywood productions, but the monster craze truly exploded in the 1960s United States. As Henry Jenkins points out, "monster culture began with the sale of old B-movies to local television stations as a syndication package in the late 1950s and early 1960s." As they invaded households through the screens of family TV sets, early film monsters were repackaged as "good clean fun for school children," who happily devoured them and became active monster fans. These young fans, notes Jenkins, "did not fear the monsters; they wanted to possess and be possessed by them."[45] This family-friendly take on monstrosity found an enduring expression in the 1962 hit novelty song "Monster Mash," in which Dracula, the Wolfman, and other monsters convene to perform the titular dance, which becomes a bona fide "graveyard smash."[46]

At the epicenter of monster fandom were magazines such as *Famous Monsters of Filmland*. Their editors softened the monsters' edges by showing how they were constructed and by explaining the magic of special effects. By making them accessible and acceptable, they gave children and young people a new opportunity to engage with monstrosity and otherness, as artfully captured in Emil Ferris's graphic novel *My Favorite Thing is Monsters*.[47] At the same time, the magazines promoted what Bob Rehak has called new *object practices*, enticing a "playful but fiercely acquisitive approach to horror."[48] Monsters became something to be collected—either as photographs, hobby model kits, or ready-made plastic toys.

Although monster culture has been studied most extensively in the US context, similar developments took place in other cultures. In China and India, the demons and monsters of regional mythologies were made accessible for family viewing in late-1980s TV adaptations of *Journey to the West* and *Mahabharat*, respectively. Out of all non-Western monster cultures, it is the Japanese one that has had the widest and most long-lasting impact.[49] Following in the footsteps of *kaiju* monster movies like 1954's *Godzilla*, the *Ultraman* TV series started production in 1966 and was almost immediately dubbed into English and shown in the United States.

According to the critic and philosopher Hiroki Azuma, the intermingling of US and Japanese influences brought forth a specific kind of engagement with popular culture, which he dubs *database consumption*. In his view, post-1990s Japanese popular culture is no longer organized around "grand," overarching narratives but rather around ever-expanding databases of characters and settings. Pop culture fans (*otakus*) enthusiastically consume nuggets from these databases, including nonnarrative merchandise such as toys.[50]

Monsters have proved to be ideal items for consumption. They travel well between cultures and come in all kinds of forms, allowing for striking and attractive designs. Many monsters are in the public domain, which allows them to be perpetually reimagined and resold. A wonderful example is the late-1980s Matchbox-produced toy line Monster in My Pocket, which gathered creatures from myth and popular culture (plus an occasional dinosaur) into an expanding roster of numbered creatures that could be added to one's collection (see figure 1.4). The back of the package reads:

> Now you can collect the greatest monsters of all time and, best of all, they'll fit in your pocket. Since the beginning of time, man has battled monsters and great monster legends existed everywhere. Now you can learn the facts about the greatest real monsters of all time . . . The more you know about these real monsters, the more fun it is to collect, trade, and play with them.[51]

The repeated use of the expression "real monsters" reads like an attempt to reconnect the tiny plastic toys to the awe and horror of sublime monstrosity. At the same time, the final sentence suggests that these "real" monsters of legend have been turned into harmless effigies you can keep in your

FIGURE 1.4
A Monster in My Pocket retail package from 1990. (Photo courtesy of the Strong, Rochester, New York.)

pocket—or, alternatively, in a "monster keeper tote bag" you could get (along with other goodies) for paying five dollars to join the "Monsters Collectors Club." Monster in My Pocket was eventually eclipsed by the enormous success of another entertainment product with pockets and monsters in its name: *Pokémon*. Starting as a 1996 role-playing video game, it has since become an omnipresent media franchise. Its monsters are inspired by the *yōkai* (helpful or mischievous spirits) of Japanese folklore but turned into "data-fied" private property that can be counted, compared, and classified.[52]

The database consumption logic resonates throughout video games, which largely rely on databases and—as noted by Janet Murray—arouse "encyclopedic expectation."[53] According to monster scholar Peter Dendle, the encyclopedic approach "has a flattening and demythologizing effect for creatures whose power ostensibly lies in their mystery."[54] At the same time, though, it has greatly contributed to the popularization and multiplication of monsters. As Anne Allison concluded from her ethnographic fieldwork in Japan, "the 'monster economy' laid out by *Pokémon* serves simultaneously as template for, and corrective to, conditions of millennial capitalism in Japan today."[55] The monsters might have lost much of their mystery, but they have also permeated much of our everyday experience.

SIMULATING THE ENEMY

In the nineteenth and twentieth centuries, efforts to contain monstrosity were bolstered by the spread of statistics, bureaucratic administration, and computer technology. Quantification, calculation, and data processing became a favored way of engaging with the challenges facing both individuals and societies. The sociologist Ulrich Beck has described this development as a shift toward a *risk society*. In his view, premodern societies tended to conceptualize adversity in terms of threats that were uncertain, unexpected, and divinely ordained. Modern societies, on the other hand, conceptualize them in terms of risks that can be statistically calculated and reasoned about.[56] The history of risk calculation can, in fact, be traced back to marine insurance policies. In one of the earliest preserved insurance contracts, sealed in 1350, a merchant insured a shipload of wheat from Sicily to Tunis, "assuming all risks, perils, and fortune . . . from acts of God, man, or the sea."[57] The insurance rates would vary based on weather conditions and other risk factors, making the adventurous business of seafaring more predictable.

The urge to reduce uncertainty and foresee future events has been especially strong in the military. One way of doing so is wargaming, which originated in the late eighteenth and early nineteenth centuries when Prussian army officers started to design (and play) mock tabletop battles for both training and entertainment. To create functional models of battle, they had to assign properties to various types of units and terrain—and in the process created the first military simulations. Already in the 1820s, Prussian wargames used dice rolls to simulate uncertainty and numerical points (predecessors to *hit points*) to represent the capacity of units to withstand damage.[58] As discussed in the next chapter, wargaming later directly influenced tabletop RPGs and video games.

Another strand of influence comes from Cold War–era military projects and from cybernetics, the dominant intellectual paradigm behind them. The technological advances at the heart of video games—general-purpose digital computing, real-time interactive interfaces, and graphic displays—were to a large extent bankrolled by the US military. According to technoculture scholar Patrick Crogan, video games inherited much of the "military technoscientific legacy." Not all video games are straightforward military propaganda (only a few are), but many adopted conceptual elements of Cold War doctrine, including what Crogan describes as "the impulse to model phenomena by hypothetically extending and extrapolating [their] future to see how that future may be predicted, modified, and controlled."[59]

The legacy is twofold: while Cold War science and engineering produced technologies designed to control and simulate conflict situations, the Cold War military ideology saw the whole world through the lens of conflict. The information scholar Paul N. Edwards has noted that the guiding strategic and ideological principle of the US military efforts of the Cold War era was the notion of a *closed world*—"a radically bounded scene of conflict, an inescapably self-referential space where every thought, word, and action is ultimately directed back toward a central struggle."[60] This mindset can be traced back to the very beginning of cybernetics, which emerged from Norbert Wiener's work during World War II on the anti-aircraft predictor, a machine that would dynamically anticipate the actions of an enemy bomber. Historian Peter Galison argues that "Wiener's image of the human and natural world is . . . a globalized, even metaphysical, extension of the epochal struggle between the implacable enemy from the sky and the Allies' calculating [anti-aircraft] predictor that did battle from the ground."[61] Consequently, any other being that enters the scope of the predictor is expected to be a ruthless but calculable enemy. This approach to otherness, which Galison has called *the ontology of the enemy*, is also common in video games, in which antagonism is the defining feature of existence for many, if not most, simulated entities.

Computer technology enabled the construction of miniature closed worlds populated by simulated enemies. A case in point is 1972's *Star Trek*, one of the first hit programs for mainframes and minicomputers to spread through the universities and research labs of the world.[62] In this text-only, turn-based tactical game, the player controls the starship

Enterprise, which moves across a grid-based space map and fights invading Klingon warships with phasers or photon torpedoes. The humanoid yet monstrous species of the Klingon offered a convenient, hostile other that could be read as a stand-in for Cold War America's Soviet foes.

Military models and simulations of reality, in general, were designed to attain "total control over a world reduced to calculable, mechanical operations."[63] Such simulations require that everything within them adheres to a unifying computational logic. To be operational, the qualities of simulated entities therefore need to be translated into numbers or algorithms. As McKenzie Wark has pointed out, "the real violence of gamespace is its dicing of everything analog into the digital, cutting continuums into bits." Such violence, Wark argues, "has nothing to do with brightly colored explosions or mounting death counts, but with the decision by digital fiat on where everything belongs and how it is ranked."[64] Digital technology boosted the ongoing efforts to build databases, dispel mysteries, and document the undocumented. This applies to video game monsters, too. The omnipresence of conflict in Cold War–era discourse and popular culture created a demand for antagonists, including monstrous ones. At the same time, the imperative of simulation was applied even to fantastic beings.

It is telling that when game scholar Espen Aarseth set out to illustrate the difference between literary fiction and video games, he picked the example of a dragon, a classic monstrous creature. More specifically, he compares a literary specimen—Smaug from Tolkien's *The Hobbit*—with the one encountered in the massively multiplayer online role-playing game (MMORPG) *EverQuest*:

One dragon is clearly fictional, but the other is simulated. One is there to read about, or watch on a TV or movie screen, the other is there to be played with. One is made solely of signs, the other of signs and a dynamic model that will specify its behavior and respond to our input. It is this model behavior that makes it different from a fiction, since we can get to know the simulation much more intimately than we come to know the fiction. . . . Simulations allow us to test their limits, comprehend causalities, establish strategies, and effect changes, in ways clearly denied us by fictions, but quite like in reality. We can't have our way with fictions, but with games, we may.[65]

For a monster to be interactive and properly function in a video game world, its behaviors, properties, and interdependencies with other objects must be unambiguously specified. In direct contradiction to Kristeva's articulation of sublime monstrosity that resists becoming an object, the dragon has become a target of our agency—it is here for us to explore and play with. As soon as we can comprehend its behavior, we can predict its future actions, come up with a strategy, and eventually defeat it. By simulating monstrosity, we are also containing it.

BUGS AND DAEMONS

The critique of the military-scientific roots of video games, while valid and necessary, runs the risk of overstating rational approaches to technology at the expense of affective ones. While the former paints computers as instruments of calculation and simulation, the latter might view them as mysterious, magical machines. Some programs are, after all, meant to produce unpredictable or astounding outcomes. A good example is *The Game of Life*, an algorithm introduced in 1970 by the mathematician John Conway and immediately written up as a computer program.[66] It is not a conventional game but rather a so-called "cellular automaton" that generates complex patterns by imposing a handful of simple rules on "cells" organized in a two-dimensional grid. The "player" provides the initial state but does not interact with the process when it is running; instead, they just observe the lifelike evolutions and extinctions that unfold on the screen. *The Game of Life*, as well as other examples of procedural generation or generative art, may evoke a sense of *computational sublime*, defined by Jon McCormack and Alan Dorin as "the instilling of simultaneous feelings of pleasure and fear in the viewer of a process realized in a computing machine."[67] In other words, it is the experience of raw, overwhelming computer magic.

If we step even further away from the rational view of computers, we may see them as homes to another kind of life: supernatural beings. In his exploration of early radio and television cultures, Jeffrey Sconce has pointed out that the astonishing liveness of electronic media and the ethereal nature of signal transmission have led some people to believe that radio and television were home to ghosts and spirits.[68] Although mostly relegated to the realms of psychosis, this belief underlines the fundamental strangeness of electronic technology and provides enduring and powerful metaphors. The term "ghosting," for example, continues to refer to the appearance of a mismatched shadow image due to signal distortion. Similarly, the agency of the computer has also been attributed to monstrous creatures—among them *bugs* and *daemons*.[69]

In common computing jargon, a bug is an error in code that produces incorrect or unexpected behavior. According to a piece of computer folklore, the term was coined on September 9, 1947, when the Harvard Mark II computer malfunctioned because of an actual moth, discovered by the team led by the computing pioneer Grace Hopper. The moth has been preserved for posterity in her notes, taped to a logbook page. This story, however, disregards the fact that engineers had already used the term in the nineteenth century. In 1878, Thomas Edison wrote of bugs in a letter to a fellow inventor, describing them as "little faults and difficulties."[70] In fact, the word in its contemporary meaning of "insect" only surfaced in the seventeenth century. Before that, it had referred to devils, fiends, or evil in general, a meaning that is still preserved in the compound *bugbear*.[71] The etymology underlines the fact that a bug can be understood conceptually as a malevolent entity that produces anomalies and subverts the intended function of a device; it represents a machine's resistance to the operator, and the resulting loss of control.[72] Similarly, the notion of the *gremlin* originated in the lore of pre–World War II fighter pilots, who blamed these fictional creatures for unexpected technical flaws on their airplanes.[73]

The other figure is that of the demon, or daemon.[74] Although Christian demonology paints demons as undisputed servants of evil, historians of science Jimena Canales and Markus Krajewski tell a history that is more interested in their functional properties. In Greek mythology, Canales and Krajewski point out, demons served as mediators between material and spiritual phenomena.[75] The figure of the demon later entered the scientific discourse when nineteenth-century physicists James

Clarke Maxwell and William Thomson (also known as Lord Kelvin) employed them in their thought experiments about thermodynamics. The demon of the Maxwell-Thomson tradition was an invisible yet nimble being who could manipulate atoms at will—"an attentive agent lying in wait in order to serve."[76] Inspired by this usage in physics, 1970s computer engineers started to use the term, spelled *daemon*, to denote "background processes which worked tirelessly to perform system chores."[77] Perhaps the best-known example is the MAILER-DAEMON, which tirelessly delivers email messages.[78]

The metaphors of bugs and daemons allow us to make sense of computers by individuating and personifying the agency of the machine.[79] While bugs disturb us with unexpected and faulty operations, daemons package it in a predictable, contained form. Bugs (meaning errors) are somewhat difficult to imagine as intentionally designed video game monsters as they might altogether prevent the player from interacting with the game. As we will see in chapter 4, game designers can nevertheless invoke awe and terror by creating the illusion that a monster breaks the program but remaining in control of player experience.

Most video game monsters can be, however, likened to daemons. As an example, we can look at the 1983 action game *Atic Atac*. In the game, the protagonist (a serf, a knight, or a wizard) navigates a haunted, maze-like castle and its dungeons. Each room remains quiet for the first few seconds after a player has entered it, creating a false sense of comfort. Soon, monsters—such as bats, jellies, ghosts, jack-o'-lanterns, or medusas—spawn out of thin air and frantically move about, dealing damage when they touch the hero (see

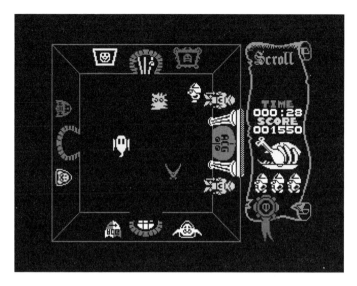

FIGURE 1.5
A ghost, a bat, and a spiky thing in *Atic Atac* (1983).

figure 1.5). A monster can be destroyed once hit by the protagonist's throwing weapon—but another critter will soon
take its place. *Atic Atac*'s monsters make the place feel alive,
and their simple movement embodies machine agency. At the
same time, they are constrained by the capabilities of the hardware; for the program to run smoothly, no more than three
monsters can be present in a room simultaneously. These creatures are algorithmic servants of the game designer, invoked by
the game's code to repetitively throw themselves against the
player, provide a dose of challenge and entertainment, perish,
and respawn if needed. The baddies of *Atic Atac* are cute rather
than transgressive, but even the enemies that are portrayed
as literal demons, like the Cacodemons of *Doom*, exhibit the

mechanical servitude of computer daemons.[80] They might be animated by magic, but it is contained magic.

I started this chapter by recounting my unexpected experience when playing *Bloodborne*. The game transported me into a Gothic world of ruin and mystery and confronted me with majestic, unsettling, and awe-inspiring monsters. But each victorious battle—while enormously exhilarating—diminished this mystery, reminding me that the abominations are just mechanical daemons, contained in a database and designed to be defeated. When I was given the choice whether to fight Ebrietas, Daughter of the Cosmos, I passed so that I could savor the experience of her sublime monstrosity. At this one moment, I went against a fundamental mechanic of the game (and possibly most monster-themed games), which rewards killing monsters with resources and trophies.

Much of theoretical literature on monsters highlights their sublime nature, but experiences of sublime monstrosity are quite rare in video games. The previous sections have presented two important reasons for this. For one, games follow in the footsteps of other entertainment media that have commodified fearsome creatures and turned them into ubiquitous playthings—while also reproducing existing stereotypical monster representations. Second, by using the technology and the intellectual framework designed to reduce uncertainty and predict enemy movements, games turn monsters into simulated entities that need to be specified and encoded. The following chapter shows how the tendency for contained and objectified monstrosity played out in the history of tabletop RPGs and arcade games and how it became engrained in one of the classic structuring principles in game design—the player vs. environment formula.

2

PLAYER VS. ENVIRONMENT

'Tis thy duty to help rid Akalabeth of the foul beasts which infest it, while trying to stay alive![1]
—from the manual of the computer role-playing game *Akalabeth* (1980)

In 2002, the US nonfiction writer Gerard Jones published a book entitled *Killing Monsters: Why Children Need Fantasy, Super Heroes, and Make-Believe Violence*, which sought to dispel the moral panic around violent genre fiction and video games.[2] Fifteen years later, I picked it up to see how a mainstream publication covers the topic of my research. To my surprise, I did not find any examples of individual video game monsters being killed—mostly, the book used "killing monsters" as shorthand for violent gameplay. By 2002, killing monsters seems to have become so ordinary that it was considered a default type of video game action.

Game scholars agree that fighting monsters is a cornerstone of many game genres. In the *Understanding Games* textbook, Simon Egenfeldt-Nielsen, Jonas Heide Smith, and Susana Tosca admit that "in the eyes of many nongamers, killing monsters is what most games are all about."[3] Game design textbooks concur. In *Patterns in Game Design*, Staffan Björk and Jussi Holopainen observe that "many games have game elements that portray people or monsters that try and hinder players' goals," while concluding that "typical ways of overcoming *enemies* are by *elimination* (most often in the form of *aim & shoot*)."[4]

But what seems so natural in today's games is, in fact, a relatively recent trend. There were few monsters in games before the advent of fantasy RPGs and computerized entertainment in the 1970s.[5] The previous chapter presented some of the factors that contributed to their proliferation, such as the rise of monster culture and the conflict-centered Cold War discourse. If we focus on the history of game design and game mechanics more specifically, monsters' invasion into ludic spaces coincides with the introduction of a particular mode of engagement that was retrospectively labeled as *player vs. environment* gameplay. This chapter explores the roots of this model by focusing on two of its foundational examples: *Dungeons & Dragons* (*D&D*) and *Space Invaders*. I argue that these games provided blueprints for the objectification and containment of monsters in the video game medium. My aim is not to provide exhaustive primary histories of these titles, but to revisit the moment when the design conventions that we now take for granted were still in the making—and to highlight the connections between the player vs. environment model and the cultural trends and ideologies of the period.

The earliest documented use of the term *player vs. environment* dates to the 1993 edition of the *Handbook of Management Games* by Chris Elgood.[6] When defining the subcategory of management simulations, Elgood notes that they are characterized by the "absence of direct human opponents, the challenge being 'player versus environment' rather than 'player versus player.'"[7] In the late 1990s, those terms resurfaced in online discussions about multiplayer online RPGs.[8] Although both modes of play had already existed, these online games were among the first to systematically combine them, and the distinction became useful for fans who wanted to express their preference for either mode. In 2002, a strategy guide for the hit online RPG *Dark Age of Camelot* explicitly defined player vs. environment (or PvE) gameplay as "combat where the enemy is a Monster (rather than another player)."[9]

I will use the term *player vs. environment* to refer to gameplay situations where a player or players control characters in a simulated environment and are confronted with sets of obstacles and enemies that are controlled by a third party, which can be either a human referee or a piece of computer software.[10] The term tends to be used in contrast to *player vs. player* gameplay, a situation in which players primarily compete against each other. The player vs. environment model is especially typical for single-player action and role-playing video games, including *Space Invaders* as well as more contemporary titles such *The Last of Us* or *The Witcher 3*.[11] The number of players is, however, not a defining feature of player vs. environment games. Chess, for example, remains a player vs. player game, even when a single human plays against an opponent that is simulated by a computer. A co-op role-playing campaign, on the other hand, has more than a single player and involves beating enemies and overcoming obstacles designed and controlled by a third party (the "game master" or "dungeon master"), and thus qualifies as a player vs. environment situation. Some games employ a combination of the two modes:

League of Legends, for example, is primarily a match between two teams of players, but both of them also fight computer-controlled monsters.[12]

Player vs. environment games can be considered newer than the player vs. player type. The 1971 scholarly compendium *The Study of Games* offers granular typologies of dimensions and structural elements of common, nondigital games (such as chess, Scrabble, or poker) but contains no mention of player vs. environment play.[13] Few nondigital player vs. environment games were publicly released prior to the 1974 release of *D&D*, with the exception of Avalon Hill's *Outdoor Survival* from 1972.[14] On several occasions, embryonic iterations of this type of gameplay appeared in early computer games for mainframes and minis. Judging by its influence on arcade game design, 1962's space-themed shooter game *Spacewar!* might seem like a good candidate, but despite its epic-sounding title, it only featured player vs. player duels.[15] The player vs. environment configuration was later explored in the strategy and resource management games such as 1971's *Oregon Trail* or 1972's *Star Trek*.[16] In both of these games, the computer was programmed to simulate a hostile environment, be it the American frontier or Klingon-dominated space. Nevertheless, the potential audience for such games was minuscule until the introduction of home computers in the second half of the decade.

DUNGEONS & DRAGONS, OR DICE & DATABASES

Few texts have influenced contemporary monster culture as much as the early rulebooks of *Dungeons & Dragons*, its very title betraying a fascination with hostile environments and hostile monsters.[17] Although it evolved into a more free-form role-playing experience, the game originated in the miniature wargame culture.[18] In the 1960s, several player groups started introducing fantasy elements, including magic and monsters, into medieval miniature wargaming.[19] There were two main reasons. First, supernatural creatures and events allowed for more attractive and varied gameplay. Second, fantasy literature, including *The Lord of the Rings*, was becoming immensely popular in the United States, especially among the fans of genre literature who made up much of the wargaming community. Incidentally, Tolkien's meticulous approach to world-building, which had foreshadowed the encyclopedic impulse typical of video game design, provided convenient inspiration for creating role-playing scenarios.[20]

Coauthored by Gary Gygax and Dave Arneson and released in 1974 by Tactical Studies Rules (TSR), *D&D* was the first commercially published tabletop RPG, allowing players to take on the roles of adventurers that embark on fantasy campaigns into dungeons and wilderness to confront monsters and uncover treasures and mysteries (see figure 2.1). Although it did not require a computer, *D&D* was, to a large extent, a *computational* game, reliant on algorithms and databases.[21] It started as an expansion to an existing medieval-themed miniature wargame called *Chainmail* and inherited the latter's emphasis on "realistic" combat. *D&D*'s monsters therefore had to be integrated in the game's simulated world on an appropriate scale and had to engage in combat according to an existing ruleset for skirmishes among humans. As *D&D* historian Jon Peterson has put it:

> [A] game places different demands on the elements of the fantasy genre than literary usages do. As the distinctions

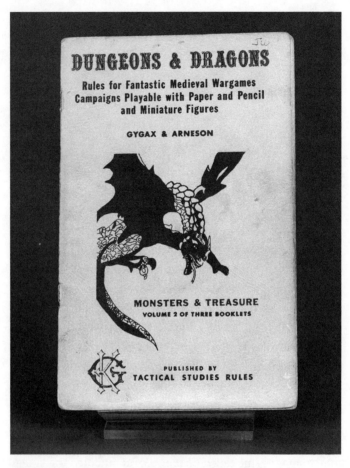

FIGURE 2.1

The *Monsters & Treasure* booklet, a part of the 1974 "white box" edition of *D&D*. (Photo courtesy of the Strong, Rochester, New York.)

between fantastic creatures grew more precise, and their characteristics became more definite, they gained a certain amount of realism: *Dungeons & Dragons* needed to render fantastic creatures realistically enough to be simulated.[22]

Monsters could not remain vaguely "outstanding" like the monster god Marduk of the Mesopotamian myth—they had to have precise statistics, or *stats*.

In the 1974 original "white box" edition, the *D&D* monster database occupied a part of a booklet called *Monsters & Treasure* but later became its own volume—the *Monster Manual*, whose inaugural 1979 version was attributed solely to Gary Gygax.[23] As Sarah Stang and Aaron Trammell point out, the manual created a new type of *ludic bestiary*, "a formula that brings together image, culture, and statistics to produce monsters in the game's world."[24] There is a certain paradox, or even folly, in the way that *D&D* meticulously simulated battles with fantastic monsters that never existed, and endowed the creatures with statistics and quasi-zoological descriptions. In effect, the *D&D* publications were arguably the first in history to describe such a wide range of monsters in such detail, surpassing the bestiaries and demonologies of yore and becoming a pinnacle of contained monstrosity.

The 1974 edition included a *Monster Reference Table* of about fifty monsters, each of which was assigned armor class, movement distance per turn (measured in inches), hit points, and potential loot.[25] This initial roster adopted, transformed, and extended the monster lore of fantasy literature, ancient mythology, and contemporary monster culture. When playing *D&D*, one could cross paths with Orcs, goblins, Trolls, giants, skeletons, zombies, manticores, minotaurs, djinns, or vampires. Although some beasts had individual weaknesses or special attacks, all of them were extracted from their original context and made to fit into one matrix of mathematical rules, which determined outcomes of game events through a combination of random dice rolls and fixed stats.

Predating Aarseth's *EverQuest* example, mentioned in the previous chapter, the following excerpt from the 1974 *D&D* rulebook shows a simulated dragon in action, highlighting the calculations performed as battles are being played out:

> A "Very Old" 11 Hit Dice Red Dragon is encountered asleep in its cavernous lair. Three fighters creep in and strike to subdue. All three hit, scoring respectively 2, 3, and 6 points, or 11 points total. 11 ratioed over 66 (the number of hit points the Dragon can absorb before being killed or in this case subdued) is 1/6th or 17%. The referee checks to determine if the Dragon is subdued and rolls over 17 on the percentile dice. The Dragon is not subdued, and a check is then made to see whether he will bite or use his breath weapon during the second melee round. The result indicates he will breathe. The attackers strike again and once more all hit for a total of 12 points. The Dragon breathes and as none make their saving throws the attackers are all killed for they take 66 points of damage from Dragon fire.[26]

Dragons (especially golden ones) are among the toughest foes in the rulebook, intended as rare encounters for high-level player characters. Unlike many other monsters, they can be defeated not only by killing them, but also by subduing them. But despite the dragon's special status, it is clearly objectified and turned into a plaything. A subdued dragon can be commanded as a player's pet bodyguard or sold to other players or on the open market. To paraphrase Aarseth, "we may have our way" with this beast.[27]

THE MONSTER IS A MONSTER

Early versions of *D&D* firmly and explicitly represented monsters as objects of player action. Moreover, the game assumed that every being one encountered was a monster. This led to an intriguing terminological confusion over what the term monster really meant. As the 1979 *Monster Manual* put it:

> The term "monster" is used throughout this work in two manners. Its first, and most important, meaning is to designate any creature encountered—hostile or otherwise, human, humanoid, or beast. Until the encountering party determines what they have come upon, it is a monster. The secondary usage of the term is in the usual sense: a horrible or wicked creature of some sort.[28]

The word monster thus referred both to gameplay function and representational quality. In effect, any nonplayer creature was by default considered a monster, and being a monster was the default mode of being "other" within the game—a configuration that bears eerie resemblance to the *ontology of the enemy*. As Matt Horrigan has pointed out in his critique of *D&D* combat rules, the monstrous opponent "seems to exist not for their own purpose but rather to provide the service of actualizing the [player] self as an agent meeting a challenge."[29] The monsters were not only objectified, but also designed as inferior to men and other selected humanoids, who—unlike monsters—could gain experience, level up, and improve their stats.[30] In the 1979 *Dungeon Master's Guide*, Gygax strongly discourages players from playing as monsters, because the game is—in his view—"unquestionably humanocentric" and "heavily weighted towards mankind."[31]

The depictions of individual monsters in *D&D*, Stang and Trammell note, reflect the biases of its authors, and particularly Gygax, a "40-year-old, married, Christian, White male insurance underwriter with a passion for wargames and science fiction."[32] Gygax, in turn, drew inspiration from white male fantasy and pulp writers such as Tolkien or Robert E. Howard.[33] It is, then, unsurprising to find problematic representations of gender and race. In the 1974 version, the only women depicted in the booklet are "witches," a "medusa," and a topless "exotic amazon." A 1978 module introduced the Drow, a fantasy race that combines both racial and gender stereotypes. The Drow were portrayed as dark-skinned elves who were evil in contrast to the good, light-skinned ones. Moreover, the Drow lived in a matriarchal society, ruled by a monstrous spider queen who, incidentally, also enjoyed appearing as an "exquisitely beautiful female."[34]

Beyond individual representations, *D&D* allowed players to confront a hostile world in a way that resonated with Gygax's job in insurance and that was familiar to the game's initial audience of American, white, middle-class players—by turning risk into capital. As animal studies scholar Matthew Chrulew has put it, creatures in *D&D* "are defined and quantified according to the game mechanics in methods that reflect and fetishize the technocratic operative modes of late capitalist societies."[35] Dead monsters are converted into experience points and loot, which provide gameplay advantage. Moreover, monsters are in limitless supply, revealing that for all the supposed realism of combat, the ecology of these simulated fantastic worlds was entirely unrealistic.[36] The rulebooks suggested distributing monsters in the game world in a way that offered adequate challenge to both low-level and experienced parties. Weaker monsters would occupy the upper levels of the dungeon, while the stronger ones lurked below. This leveled the playing field between the players and the enemies, suggesting that each monster could potentially be defeated.

To allow this structure of gameplay, monsters were almost completely *virtualized*, or disconnected from a tangible material representation.[37] Although *D&D* descended from miniature wargaming, the use of miniatures was considered optional, providing an illustration or visual aid rather than a one-to-one representation of the game world.[38] The game state was instead represented on paper and in the shared discourse among the players and the referee. The disconnection between miniatures as physical objects and virtual simulated monsters removed the limits to the number of monsters than could be met and defeated. A good example of this virtualization is the concept of *wandering monsters*, who would appear with a certain probability in a certain region, signaling the statistical risk of traversing hostile lands.

ALWAYS LOOKING FOR MORE MONSTERS

With its business model reliant on selling additional campaign modules, *D&D*—as well as competitors like *Tunnels & Trolls*—thrived on the demand for more adventures and more monsters. To quote Chrulew, fantasy RPGs "plunder history, literature, science, and mythology, portraying and playing with all."[39] The *D&D* ruleset was abstract and open enough to support a potentially infinite monster database, and the game grew to absorb narratives and creatures from myth and popular culture, converting them into game content. In the 1976 expansion *Gods, Demi-Gods & Heroes*, even deities received their stats.[40] The monster library expanded geographically, too. Creatures like Owlbear and Bulette, introduced in the mid-1970s, were based on cheap plastic toys imported from Taiwan, which might have in turn been knock-offs of *Ultraman*, the Japanese kaiju TV show, highlighting *D&D*'s connections to international monster cultures.[41] In 1983, the *Ravenloft* module introduced a quasi-Eastern European setting of Barovia, inspired by vampire narratives and Gothic fiction.[42] A third-party brochure *Monsters of Myth & Legend* from 1984 offered a roster of creatures from six cultures (Native American, Aboriginal Australian, Chinese, Greek, Irish, and Norse), and in 1985, *D&D* introduced the campaign setting *Oriental Adventures*, inspired by a patchwork of Chinese, Japanese, Korean, and Southeast Asian myth and folklore. The setting was later—unsurprisingly and rightfully—criticized for its orientalist outlook.[43]

The notion of an ever-expandable library of monsters opened the doors to plentiful DIY creatures. Scrappy, unofficial booklets like 1977's *All the Worlds' Monsters* provided hundreds of fan-made monsters for *D&D* and competing game systems. As the book's editors point out: "Limited as it is, this still is an endless book. . . . We always are looking for more monsters."[44] Most of these monsters were designed not to evoke awe and terror, but to entertain players and playfully explore the possibilities of roleplaying systems. That was also the case with some of *D&D*'s most famous original creatures. The Gelatinous Cube, for instance, was a monster shaped by the game's topological rules—it measured ten feet on each side to fit into *D&D*'s standard ten-by-ten-foot dungeon corridors. The Beholder was a levitating orb with one giant eye and ten eye stalks with additional eyes, each of which could cast a different powerful spell (see figure 2.2).[45] Its appeal stemmed from the incongruous combination of its grotesque appearance and its devastating powers. *D&D*

FIGURE 2.2
Beholder Eye Tyrant, an official *D&D* miniature from the 2009 Dangerous Delves series. (Photo by Jaroslav Švelch Sr.)

players enjoyed making up such weird and comical monsters; one of the fan-made bestiaries, entitled *Weird Works*, included a huge blue Smurf Giant, as well as a Lint Quasi-Elemental, which attacked by "forcing itself into one's navel—its natural habitat."[46]

Thanks to the overlap between wargaming and early tech subcultures, *D&D* had an immediate impact on computer and video games.[47] The first *D&D*-inspired computer games—such as *dnd* for the PLATO platform—surfaced around 1975, almost simultaneously with the pen-and-paper original. The first commercial computer RPGs, such as the *Ultima* and *Wizardry* series, launched in the early 1980s, soon after home computers became available on the mass market. In these adaptations, monsters were even more prominent than in their tabletop counterparts. Due in part to technological limitations, these titles—sometimes called "hack-and-slash" by the contemporary press—emphasized exploration and combat, the latter of which could be adapted from *D&D* in a straightforward fashion.[48]

Without a human referee, the repertoire and the behaviors of the monsters were determined in the code and data files of the games, unambiguous and nonnegotiable. At this point, monsters were usually the only computer-controlled entities in the game world and motivated the majority of player action. The quantity of monsters therefore became an important sales point. The packaging of the 1980 title *Akalabeth*, a predecessor to the *Ultima* series, prominently advertises "10 different hi-res monsters" as its primary selling point.[49] The game's advertising implies both the challenge and the promise of overcoming it, because, unsurprisingly, the player must defeat multiple exemplars of these ten

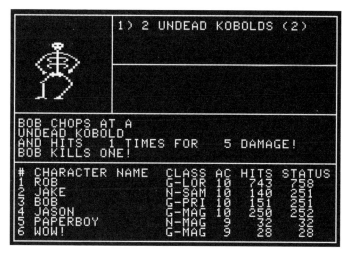

FIGURE 2.3
A party fights a group of undead in *Wizardry: Proving Grounds of the Mad Overlord* (1981).

monsters to finish the game. The manual of 1981's *Wizardry: Proving Grounds of the Mad Overlord* promised "hundreds of monsters," and delivered in spades.[50] Given the automation of dice-rolling and hit calculation, combat could unfold much faster, albeit with less nuance and surprise than when playing with a human referee. In addition, *Wizardry* allowed one player to control a whole party of adventurers at once and take on greater challenges (see figure 2.3).

Both *Ultima* and *Wizardry* followed the example of *D&D* and called *any* enemy a monster, even when they were human or humanoid antagonists. Today, the rank-and-file cannon fodder enemies in video games are often called *mobs*. The term, shortened from *mobiles*, dates to *MUD* or *Multi-User Dungeon*, the foundational online multiplayer role-playing computer game cowritten in 1978 by Richard Bartle, then a student at the University of Essex. Bartle remembers that when building the object database for the game, he needed to distinguish static objects from those that could move or change states. He called the latter *mobiles*. Initially an internal label, it spread thanks to players who peeked into the game's code.[51] As a dictionary of "MUDspeke" jargon puts it, mobiles are "a class of MUD-controlled inhabitants of The Land which (usually) wander around. Most can be killed reasonably easily, but some are very nasty. . . . A small percentage are friendly."[52] By the early 2000s, the abbreviation *mob* displaced the original term, and, likely thanks to the word's alternative meaning of *horde*, spread among communities around online RPGs like *EverQuest*.[53] Although Bartle's original category encompassed more than just enemies or monsters, today's usage of the term offers another variation on the *ontology of the enemy* by suggesting the equation between mobility and hostility.

THE INEXORABLE DESCENT OF *SPACE INVADERS*

The fast-paced attack of the aliens in *Space Invaders* seems a far cry from the statistical monsters of *D&D*. However, the arcade title, released in 1978 by Taito, solidified the player vs. environment template in the arcade space by presenting monsters as hostile moving targets. *Space Invaders* was neither the first shooter game nor the first monster-themed arcade game. Aim-and-shoot gameplay goes back to darts, funfair shooting galleries, and automated mechanical and electromechanical shooting games.[54] In the nineteenth and early twentieth centuries, however, one did not shoot at monsters, at least not in the narrow sense of fantastical creatures. These games either employed an abstract carnival aesthetic or featured real-life themes of hunting or warfare.[55] Looking into collections of vintage American shooting targets, we can see an array of "others" that were deemed suitable to shoot at, such as card suits, disembodied clown heads, animals, or Native Americans, reminding us of the speciesism and racism in enemy representations.[56]

In the 1960s and 1970s, arcade machine manufacturers started responding to the surge of monster culture. In the United States, Midway's 1967 electromechanical game *Monster Gun* featured "20 scary moving targets" rotating along two concentric disks.[57] The targets were disembodied cartoony heads of the Frankenstein monster, as well as assorted imps and goblins. Three years later, the company launched *Invaders from Outer Space* (also known as *The Invaders*), featuring pastel-colored cartoon alien figures as targets, moving from side to side and bobbing up and down.[58] In Japan, Sega soon followed suit, producing games with identical titles, similar themes, but different monsters. Sega's *Monster Gun* (1972) featured dinosaur-inspired beasts instead of the American version's goblins, and its *Invaders* (also 1972) let the players shoot at "invaders from outer space travelling in disc-like vehicles."[59] There were also monster-themed pinball tables, going all the way back to 1950's *Flying Saucer* by Genco or 1965's *Mystery Score* by Midway.

Taito's *Space Invaders*, however, offered more than a remediation of its electromechanical predecessors. Earlier shooting games mostly functioned as tests of skill, measuring how many hits a player could score within a time limit or within a certain number of attempts. In shooting galleries, in electromechanical shooter games, and even in pre–*Space*

Invaders digital arcade games like Atari's 1975 *Anti-Aircraft*, players could compete with others for a high score or try to improve their own, but they did not have to fear the enemies. The worst harm that a target could do was to not get hit.[60] *Space Invaders* raised the stakes. Its monsters, controlled by then-novel microprocessor technology, fought back, dropping bombs on the cannon that served as the player's avatar and relentlessly descending on its position. They presented an immediate, real-time threat, resonating with the Cold War fears of nuclear conflict and airborne attacks. As Bob Rehak has pointed out: "*Space Invaders'* introduction of nonhuman others restructured screen identity, disarticulating avatarial forms from material bodies and shifting the mode of consumption from two-player dyads to solitary space."[61] *Space Invaders* offered an asymmetrical conflict with a multitude of hostile others and offered a clear formulation of the player vs. environment formula.

Although the 1972 computer strategy game *Star Trek* featured Klingon ships that could harm the player-controlled Enterprise, this concept had not yet reached the arcades. The pleasurable annihilation of invaders was in fact inspired by the 1976 Atari arcade game *Breakout*, a single-player variation of Atari's breakthrough machine *Pong*.[62] The *Space Invaders'* designer Tomohiro Nishikado sought to replicate the "sense of achievement at destroying the targets,"[63] he felt while smashing bricks in *Breakout* (see figures 2.4 and 2.5). Digital technology allowed for such pleasurable annihilation on a previously impossible scale. In the 1970 electromechanical game *Invaders from Outer Space*, for example, the targets would flip over when hit, but they always remained attached to the machinery. Destroying a virtual target in *Breakout* or *Space Invaders*, on the other hand, did not involve rearrangement of metal, plastic, or paper, but merely a change of current in the machine's circuitry.

Before settling on alien monsters, Nishikado toyed with other enemy designs:

> First, I thought of making tanks or airplanes as the targets to shoot, but it was technically hard to make airplanes look like they are actually flying. Human movement would have been easier, but I felt it would be immoral to shoot humans, even if they were bad guys. Then I heard about a movie called *Star Wars* released in the US, which was coming to Japan next year, so I came up with a game based in space which had space aliens as targets.[64]

Nishikado's explanation points to some of the reasons why monsters continue to be go-to video game enemies. First, their exaggerated features emphasize movement and action. The invaders' animated limbs and tentacles do the important job of signaling liveness that surpasses simple linear locomotion. Second, monsters make violence morally acceptable.[65] In Japan specifically, game companies were historically reluctant to include realistic violence because of the troubling memories of World War II, providing an additional impetus for using monstrous rather than human opponents.[66] Third, these games tap into an existing monster culture. By the time Nishikado designed his game, he had not actually seen *Star Wars*, but instead found inspiration in the octopus-like monsters of H. G. Wells's *War of the Worlds*, basing the now-iconic bitmaps on various sea creatures.[67]

The invaders' pixelated graphics, along with their relentless and repetitive movement, make it clear that these monsters are denizens of the machine. But are they daemons, or are they bugs? Like daemons, they can be summoned and

FIGURE 2.4
Breakout (1976) in progress. At the start of each round, there are 112 bricks to destroy.

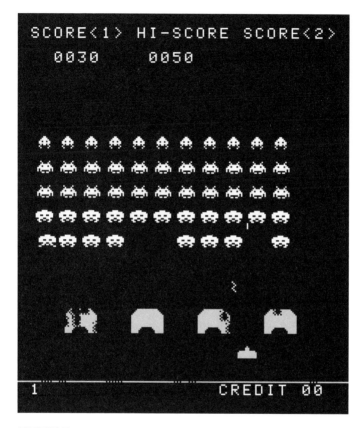

FIGURE 2.5
Space Invaders (1978) in progress. The game starts with 55 enemies on the screen.

banished almost instantaneously, offering the pleasures of fast-paced destruction. At the same time, their behavior is affected by a rather malevolent bug. The game speeds up as aliens are cleared off the screen and processing power is freed up. This was not an intentional design element, but Nishikado kept it in to step up the challenge.

Players at the time were dumbstruck by the game's audio-visual spectacle and conceptual novelty. In his 1982 reportage book on the arcade video game phenomenon, Martin Amis writes:

> I had driven toy cars, toy aeroplanes, toy submarines; I had shot toy cowboys, toy tanks, toy sharks. But I knew instantly that this was something different, something special. Cinematic melodrama blazing on the screen, infinite firing capacity, the beautiful responsiveness of the defending turret, the sting and pow of the missiles, the background pulse of the quickening heartbeat, the inexorable descent of the bomb-dumping monsters: my awesome task, to save Earth from destruction![68]

For Amis, it was the drama that was the main innovation of *Space Invaders*. Commenting on the game's legacy and its numerous copycats, he concludes that "after *Space Invaders*, we were *defending Earth*, against monsters, in sublunar skies."[69] The *Space Invaders* craze of the late 1970s triggered a major upheaval in game industry trends. At Atari, as documented by Raiford Guins, shooters replaced driving and sports games as the most profitable genre.[70] Several other seminal shooter titles were released in subsequent years, including Atari's *Asteroids* and *Centipede*, Williams's *Defender*, and Namco's *Galaga*.[71] The drama between the player and the environment was here to stay.

AVOID THE NASTIES

Regardless of the outsize influence of *D&D* and *Space Invaders*, it is important to acknowledge alternative conceptualizations of the player vs. environment formula that favor stealth or avoidance rather than direct confrontation with an enemy. Some of the 1980s titles in the "platform game" subgenre left their protagonists completely defenseless. *Manic Miner*, a 1983 British hit by Matthew Smith, stars a hapless miner named Willy who delves into the caverns under his home, inhabited by an ensemble of delightfully odd critters (see figure 2.6). According to the game's instructions, Willy must "collect all the flashing keys in the room while avoiding nasties like Poisonous Pansies and Spiders and Slime and worst of all, Manic Mining Robots."[72] Each of the monsters tirelessly follows a fixed path, like mechanical toys wound up by the programmer. Any collision with them results in instant death. The primary mechanic of the game is, ostensibly, jumping between platforms and over monsters. Successful navigation, however, requires the player to patiently observe the nasties,

FIGURE 2.6

"Eugene's Lair," one of *Manic Miner*'s (1983) most infamous caverns, featuring killer toilets and the bespectacled Eugene, inspired by Smith's coworker Eugene Evans.

learn by trial and error, and attune one's movements to the rhythm of the monsters. Unlike the aliens in *Space Invaders*, these monsters cannot be destroyed—but they can be figured out. While *Manic Miner* inspired a host of combat-free copycats, later influential platformers like *Super Mario Bros.* (1985) and *Rayman* (1995) let their protagonists dispatch monsters with various kinds of cartoon violence.[73]

Another alternative model of monster engagement was introduced by *Pac-Man*, the 1980 arcade hit designed by Toru Iwatani for Namco. To appeal to the underserved audience of women (and couples), Iwatani avoided militaristic and violent themes and built his game around the themes of food and eating. The titular protagonist must consume pellets while avoiding the four ghost monsters—named Inky, Blinky, Pinky, and Clyde for the North American release—who chase him. Intriguingly, each ghost is controlled by a different algorithm, which endows them with a rudimentary personality and distinguishes their movement patterns. The dynamic of the chase changes whenever Pac-Man eats a power pill—at that point, the ghosts become temporarily harmless, and it is Pac-Man who can eat *them* up. According to a recent recollection by Iwatani, this shifting dynamic between the protagonist and the monsters was inspired by Tom and Jerry from the eponymous animated series, who are, according to Iwatani, "quasi-enemies."[74] Just as Tom cannot definitively best Jerry (and vice versa), the ghosts of *Pac-Man* never really go away—they are just temporarily banished. In his book on the game, Alex Wade argues that the dynamic of a relentless chase "places *Pac-Man* at the genealogical head of survival games."[75] Another title with a claim to be a "first" survival game is 1981's *3D Monster Maze* by the British programmer Malcolm Evans, in which—as already mentioned in chapter 1—the protagonist must escape the titular maze while evading a Tyrannosaurus Rex.[76] Unlike *Pac-Man*, the game is played from the first-person perspective, which limits the information about the playing field and produces scary encounters with an invincible monster that takes more and more screen space as it hurries towards the player.

The avoidance-based mechanics of hide-and-seek and chase have since been adopted by a subgenre of *survival horror* games, described by Perron as "action-adventure games where the vulnerability of the player character is played out through not so powerful weapons and limited ammo and health."[77] In such games, the anticipated play strategy is usually to observe and analyze the monsters' behavior in order to avoid them. Even if they are not defeated in the sense of physical destruction, they are outsmarted and figured out, losing some or all their sublime qualities. In the end, Perron admits that even in horror games, "on the whole, a monster is to be faced."[78]

A FLOW OF MONSTERS

D&D and *Space Invaders* have exerted enormous influence on game design and popular culture. RPGs such as *D&D* started as a niche hobby but went on to have "a pervasive and ongoing impact on cultural practices and production."[79] Inspired by the success of the *Ultima* and *Wizardry* series, TSR started licensing their product to software studios, giving birth to official *D&D* adaptations like the SSI Gold Box line or, later, *Baldur's Gate*.[80] *D&D* mechanics such as hit points and character leveling have become mainstays of video game design and expanded to other genres including action games. In Japan, series like *Dragon Quest* and *Final Fantasy* built on the foundations of *Wizardry* and *Ultima* but gradually added more emphasis on narrative and character design, creating a distinct lineage of Japanese RPGs (JRPGs), in which some of the *D&D* conventions—such as random encounters or turn-based combat—persevered even longer than in their Western counterparts.[81]

Hostile moving targets have learned new tricks since the days of *Space Invaders*, but the fundamentals have remained virtually unchanged. As Krzywinska notes, "it is . . . not much of a leap from rows of space invaders marching down the screen toward a player . . . to the more visually and behaviorally complex monsters of the latest PlayStation 4 big-budget horror [games]."[82] Even one of the most recent major mechanical innovations in shooter games—the cover system popularized in 2006 by *Gears of War*—was foreshadowed in the form of *Space Invaders'* destructible bunkers.[83]

Together, *D&D* and *Space Invaders* popularized player vs. environment gameplay and provided a baseline for video game combat mechanics. Their respective strands of design conventions have also frequently cross-pollinated. One of the early games to marry *D&D* and shooter mechanics was Atari's 1985 arcade game *Gauntlet*, whose working title was *Dungeons* and which featured a team of four players exploring a castle and fighting its monstrous denizens.[84] A peek into its design documentation shows how the designers conceived of the role of monsters in player vs. environment gameplay. The outline stipulates that the "main motivation of the game will be to 'blast the jelly' out of the opposing forces (anything that moves)" and adds that "the monsters of this game have only one purpose for existing, they must attack and attempt to destroy any who trespass inside the Castle Morda-Nima."[85]

The proliferation of the player vs. environment model was fast and far-reaching. According to games and ecology scholar Alenda Y. Chang, "PvE was the de facto mode of most computer and console gaming before networked online play became commonplace."[86] (Among the important exceptions were various adaptations of popular nondigital games and contests, such as sports or racing titles.) The popularity of the model can be explained in several complementary ways. First, it resonates with traditional hero narratives—such as myths, fairy tales, Westerns, and adventure films—in which a protagonist faces a hostile environment. It provides an experience of agency and power fantasy that has since become an important selling point of video games. Second, it reflects the values of the time, such as the Cold War–era obsession with armed conflict, or the individualism typical of postwar capitalist culture, manifesting in an entrepreneurial drive to take on risk and improve one's score in a competitive environment.[87] Third, it was buttressed by computer technology, which was slowly becoming mainstream in the 1970s. The flickering of monstrous daemons on cathode-ray tube screens embodied the novelty of computer technology. The technology did not, however, directly *determine* the player vs. environment model—after all, computers are just as capable of producing the computational sublime. Rather, it proved to be an ideal tool to realize the already existing idea of simulating hostile worlds. The player vs. environment model was also a good fit for emerging consumer practices, namely the individual and private engagement with digital technology enabled by home consoles and home computers. The *Wizardry* series, for example, let one set out on a multicharacter role-playing campaign without the need for other players.

Finally, the fourth—banal but necessary—reason for the spread of player vs. environment gaming is the fact that killing monsters makes for a satisfying gameplay experience. As Krzywinska notes, "at base, monsters are convenient game mechanics."[88] To use a popular game design term, monsters keep up the *flow* of the game. The concept of flow, introduced by Mihály Csikszentmihalyi in 1975, describes the experience of an individual—be it a video game player, an artist, or a mountain climber—who becomes engrossed by a challenging but enjoyable activity. To achieve flow, the activity in question must have clear goals and provide an adequate level of challenge: easy enough to prevent anxiety and difficult enough to prevent boredom. In his compelling critique of the concept, Braxton Soderman points out that it carries significant ideological baggage:

> The flow state became the ideal that individuals could strive toward. Yet flow theory promotes ideas that align with neoliberal ideologies of individuality and the pursuit of economic growth. Ideologically, flow theory privileges individuality over social collectives, self-determination over theories of external determination, growth over stability, and action over critical examination.[89]

According to Soderman's account, Csikszentmihalyi saw his flow theory as an alternative to Marxism: a way of dealing with the feelings of alienation experienced by people in developed capitalist societies while avoiding social struggle. In effect, flow theory then suggests that "we do not need to remove (or solve) external causes of anxiety and worry, but simply change our minds and distract ourselves from these causes."[90] Soderman does not criticize flow activities themselves as much as the celebration of flow as a cure-all for social and psychological ills as well as a default solution to game design challenges. Originally a concept emerging from Csikszentmihalyi's field work, it has become "an unquestioned tool for . . . authors of design manuals," especially when explaining how to design an optimal gameplay experience.[91]

The concept and the critique of flow can be used to explain the role of monsters in player vs. environment games. Monsters (and other generic opponents) give players something to do, keep them attentive and occupied, and maintain the flow of the gameplay experience by providing clear and well-defined challenges—neither too difficult nor too easy. They provide the joy of pleasurable annihilation rewarded by numerical growth, introduced by *D&D* and *Space Invaders* and perfected by games like the *Diablo* series.[92] At the same time, they serve as a distraction from the actual threats that haunt the contemporary world, which are much more complex and lie beyond the scope of individual agency.

While flow remains an aim in much of game design, Mortensen and Jørgensen note that experiences of the sublime can arise from disruptions to flow.[93] These may include moments of extreme difficulty bordering on frustration, moments of relinquishing control to marvel at a virtual landscape, moments of highly charged emotional content that forces self-reflection, or just moments when technology fails, resulting in a glitch. All of these present openings for sublime and subversive monstrosity and I will return to them in chapter 4.

EXPENDABLE OTHERS

Let us now sum up what the player vs. environment model typically means for monsters. First, they are *hostile*, similar to enemy aircraft in Cold War–era military models. Second, they are *objectified*—they become targets of player action, usually to be defeated and turned into loot or score; sometimes, the goal is to "clear" an area of all monsters to progress or gain advantage. Third, they are *virtualized*, meaning that they can be dissociated from material objects like moving targets or miniatures. This allows them to be summoned, controlled, destroyed, and respawned in large quantities, like computer daemons. This is a significant departure from most monster narratives in other media. While Beowulf killed three monsters, a character in *Gauntlet* will kill hundreds.[94]

The simulated "environment" in the player vs. environment model is rarely an environment in a social or ecological sense, with complex webs of relationships among creatures and material objects. Following Georgia Leigh McGregor's taxonomy of the uses of video game spaces, we can understand it as a combination of "contested space" (for whose dominance the player fights against monstrous opponents) and "challenge space" (which contains various traps and other hazards).[95] *D&D* and *Space Invaders* introduced two canonical sites of video game monster encounters: underground dungeons and the outer space. Both are dark and foreboding locales adjacent to but separate from human society, inhospitable to a common understanding of nature. Besides dungeons, *D&D* took place in the wilderness, which—according to the 1974 rulebooks—"consists of unexplored land, cities and castles."[96] The books do not mention *by whom* it is unexplored, but we can assume that it is by the player party, who can therefore engage in a colonialist power fantasy of navigating and exploiting unknown lands. The following chapters will show that many later games (including the later editions of *D&D*) have added more variety and thoughtfully expanded these environments and the relationships within them, but the idea of a hostile environment remains an integral part of the player vs. environment formula.

D&D and *Space Invaders*, together with their descendants, normalized the casting of monsters as enemies that populate (rather than *inhabit*) these environments and embody their hostility. Monsters fulfil the role of what René Glas has termed *generic expendables* and what Nathan Hunt has called *utilitarian antagonists*—opponents who can be destroyed with no qualms about the implications.[97] In the words of the *Gauntlet* team, this is often their "one purpose for existing."

Throughout video game history, monsters have been used as a replacement for humans to appease rating boards concerned with virtual violence. In 1997, the studio behind the racing game *Carmaggedon* produced a so-called "alternative blood" version, in which pedestrians—the killing of whom the game rewarded—bled green liquid so that they could be interpreted as zombies.[98] But as Carly Kocurek has pointed out, these attempts to reduce game violence "may enact a different type of rhetorical violence, echoing the strategies of dehumanisation employed in propaganda campaigns."[99] In other words, using monsters as generic expendables can bolster the conviction that *any* opponent—even human or animal—is monstrous. It represents a trivialized and reductive notion of otherness defined solely by opposition and destruction. Moreover, the alternative blood examples show that there is a thin line between human and monstrous enemies. As I have argued elsewhere, even humanoid enemies in video games are "always already monsters," because they are, in essence, computational others—namely daemons—masquerading as humans.[100] This is not to say that representation does not matter. We may well expect that players experience killing opponents that are clearly human differently from killing those who are clearly monstrous. But many games choose to strip human enemies of their humanity either by presenting them as addicts, cultists, or Nazis, or by covering their faces with grotesque masks, which is the case in games like *BioShock* or *Deathloop*.[101] Such opponents can be considered at least partially monstrous on the level of audiovisual and narrative representation, too.

Monsters come in different shapes and sizes, exhibit different kinds of behaviors, and require different tactics. As Björk and Holopainen state in their textbook of game design patterns: "Games that provide many enemies can give them different abilities to support orthogonal unit differentiation, and thereby varied gameplay, or vary the environment in which these enemies are encountered."[102] In the *Last of Us* series, for example, this differentiation is clearly marked by the names given to the various types of the zombie-like enemies: Runners, Stalkers, Clickers, Bloaters, and Shamblers.[103] Clickers, for example, cannot see but have a heightened sense of hearing, and their design encourages a stealthy playstyle.[104] Within a particular category, though, video game monsters tend to be *fungible*, meaning that there are many functionally interchangeable exemplars of the same kind: a Clicker is a Clicker is a Clicker.[105]

Over the years, conventional patterns of enemy behavior have emerged and solidified; for example, hulking monsters are slow while small monsters are fast. A common critique of monster design is that it relies on a series of clichéd mechanics, leading to a mismatch between the monsters' "lore" (meaning background narratives) and their mechanics. When analyzing the representation of Dracula in the *Castlevania* series, game scholar Clara Fernández-Vara finds that "[the] digital Dracula's powers are different from those we traditionally associate with his novel or film counterparts." The in-game Dracula does not transform into a bat and does not suck blood; instead, he throws fireballs like a stereotypical video game boss. Fernández-Vara concludes that "he could be Dracula, the Mummy, or any other arch-villain for that matter." In other words, he has been "defanged."[106] Roger Luckhurst expresses the same sentiment in noting that the zombies of *Resident Evil* are divested of their zombie-specific behavior and become "merely obstructive pixels—problems to be solved—that could just as well have been rendered as demons, or aliens, or Nazis."[107] In other words, they are the same daemons wearing different masks. Just as *D&D* strove to fit all creatures into its database, so are diverse monsters cut to size to fit into the matrix of conventional video game mechanics. In the process, their idiosyncrasies may be erased and their sublime qualities contained. Overall, the success of the player vs. environment model has opened the doors for monsters, inviting an outburst of creativity and plenty of creatures to play with. At the same time, it has relegated monsters to the role of hostile enemies and constricted the possible range of their mechanical designs.

3

THE ART OF THE MONSTROUS

When I make an enemy, I treat it as an extension of myself.
—Kazunori Inoue, gameplay programmer of *Bayonetta*,
responsible for most monster behavior in the game[1]

Many video game monsters must pass a silhouette test. Creators of games as distinct as *Pokémon Gold* and *Dead Space*—a kid-friendly RPG and a gruesome horror shooter, respectively—attest that a physical outline is one of the first steps to designing a new monster. An outline of a monster is judged not only by aesthetic considerations, but also by usability requirements. The production designer of *Dead Space* speaks not just of the need for "creepy shapes that trigger something in people" but also of the necessity for silhouettes that are distinct enough, "because you have to be able to tell them apart."[2] *Pokémon* designers likewise reject any new monsters whose silhouettes look too similar to the existing ones.[3] To ensure smooth gameplay progress, the player must know who they are fighting against. Video game monstrosity may be creepy or bizarre, but it should not compromise a satisfying user experience.

The player vs. environment model, discussed in detail in the previous chapter, has become one of the most widely used structuring principles of video games. Leaning heavily on combat, the model calls for enemies that are hostile, objectified, and virtualized—and monsters are ready to play the part. Game developers therefore face a tough challenge: how to create monsters that are imposing, threatening, and mysterious but at the same time allow players to experience the satisfaction of playing against and defeating them? Juggling these two contradictory requirements requires a great deal of creative work, which is the focus of this chapter.

The chapter traces the norms and processes that shape the design of video game monsters. Its first part offers a brief excursion into archaeology and art history, showing how artists and artisans of the past have grappled with monstrosity and how they contributed to the conventions of monster design. The subsequent sections explore monster design in contemporary games, focusing primarily on *God of War*, Sony Santa Monica's 2018 entry in the eponymous series well known for its intense fantasy combat.[4] Taking cues from the rapidly developing field of game production studies, I offer a peek into the complex and interdisciplinary process of enemy design and show how monsters' representations and mechanics become contained within the parameters of game production routines, development tools, and user experience design conventions.[5]

MARVELS IN THE MARGINS

Given the omnipresence of monsters in various cultures of the world, one might think that monstrous images emerged with the first humans. The archaeologist David Wengrow, however, argues that this is not the case. Tracing the origins of what he calls "counterintuitive" and "composite" figures, he finds that depictions of nonexistent creatures are strikingly rare in the archaeological record of hunter-gatherer and early farming cultures. This does not mean that such cultures did not have monsters but that these were more likely to be represented verbally or by the means of ephemeral performance. A shaman, for instance, would wear a mask and channel a monster, but only for the duration of a ritual.[6] Monsters only became frequently depicted—and even fashionable—about six thousand years ago in the early city states of the Near East, during a period that Wengrow calls the "first age of mechanical reproduction." At that time, hybrid and composite images, such as many-limbed humans or winged mammals, started appearing on engraved stamps and cylinder seals. Wengrow attributes their origins to a novel method of abstract reasoning brought about by the growth of large-scale social formations:

> Composites thus encapsulated, in striking visual forms, the bureaucratic imperative to confront the world, not as we ordinarily encounter it—made up of unique and sentient totalities—but as an imaginary realm made up of divisible subjects, each comprising a multitude of fissionable, commensurable, and recombinable parts.[7]

Although Wengrow carefully avoids technological determinism, he does suggest that the new technologies of mechanical reproduction and the standardization of material culture allowed counterintuitive images to be stabilized, further developed, and exported to other cultures. The Near Eastern hybrids had a profound impact on the monstrous imaginary of ancient Egypt and Greece and propped up the imagination of the monster creators who came next.[8] The archeological evidence, then, suggests that the proliferation of monstrous images was tied to the emergence of new conceptual and technological tools, which introduced new possibilities—as well as limitations—of creative expression.

Monstrous art has been a site of playful experimentation, a phenomenon thoroughly explored by the art historian Michael Camille in the context of medieval Europe. In Western culture, monstrous forms were often criticized as frivolous and obscene and relegated to the fringes of legitimate art.[9] In the Middle Ages, the prime examples of monstrous imagery therefore resided, quite literally, in the margins of medieval manuscripts and on the edges of monasteries and cathedrals. As manuscript illumination established itself as a stand-alone profession in the thirteenth century, illuminators felt free to comment, subvert, and parody the content of manuscripts handed to them by scribes (see figure 3.1).[10] According to Camille, marginal drawings were not random doodles but rather images "as conscious and as instrumental as the little monsters that bleep and zig-zag across today's computer screens in similar games of scopic concentration."[11] Likewise, gargoyles adorning medieval buildings signified "spiritual control and subjugation of demonic forces," but their fantastic shapes were an attraction in themselves.[12] For Camille, the aesthetic of Romanesque and Gothic marginal monstrosity "is irrevocably linked with the capacity of the human imagination to create and combine."[13] Margins were a site of considerable creative freedom, and monsters "offered a field for technical, formal, and even iconographic experimentation."[14] Although Renaissance art temporarily discarded

FIGURE 3.1
An unnamed hybrid creature from the margins of the Ormesby Psalter from early fourteenth-century England. (MS. Douce 366, detail of folio 34v. Courtesy of the Bodleian Libraries, University of Oxford.)

monstrous experiments in favor of realism, this changed in the late fifteenth century following the discovery of Domus Aurea, a palace complex built in Rome around 64 AD.[15] Visitors to the newly unearthed site admired vibrant frescoes in which hybrid creatures grew in and out of vines and foliage; they were captivated by the "sheer mass of fantastic figures—the unabashed eruption of enticing, puzzling, mind-bending, frightening" forms.[16] Because of the mistaken assumption that the decorated rooms were underground caves, or *grottos*, their style came to be known as *grotesque*. Despite their different lineage, grotesque creatures bore many morphological similarities to their medieval counterparts. Today, the term grotesque is used to describe hybridity and deformity in general, or, in the words of Mikhail Bakhtin, to highlight a "hyperbolism of bodily images."[17]

Medieval monstrosity was rediscovered when the Romantics fell in love with the Gothic. Perhaps the most famous of all gargoyles, the *stryge* that overlooks Paris from the Notre Dame cathedral, is not a medieval sculpture but a nineteenth-century addition. By the time of the cathedral's restoration around 1850, the original gargoyles had either been removed or severely damaged, but the architect in charge of the restoration, Eugène Viollet-le-Duc, was determined to make them anew. Inspired by their medieval forebears, he personally designed hundreds of gargoyles (or, as he called them, *chimeras*) and had them carved and placed prominently around the building. At the time, many deemed his monstrous obsession excessive, like a neoclassicist architect who opined that "monsters, spikes, gargoyles, all this grotesque horde [that] makes faces at me . . . a carnivalesque charivari making an infernal din in the ears of pure and chaste harmony." Viollet-le-Duc, however, defended monsters as a pinnacle of artistic practice, asking the rhetorical question: "But are we to suppose that such creations belong only to primitive culture? Does not art exercise its functions in our day in giving verisimilitude to fictions?"[18] Despite the criticism, the gargoyles, and especially the *stryge*, became a shorthand for Notre Dame and Paris in general, in part thanks to its proliferation in ephemeral images like postcards (see figure 3.2). This way, a marginal creature asserted its authority over the city through marginal media.

As noted in the previous chapter, it is the monsters of cinema that have had the most immediate impact on video game aesthetics. Over decades, filmmakers have used a wide

FIGURE 3.2
The Stryge of Notre Dame, then brand new, in an 1853 etching by
Charles Meryon. (National Gallery of Art, Washington, DC. Reprinted
under Creative Commons CC0 1.0 license.)

repertoire of techniques to bring fantastic creatures to the screen, including masks, makeup, prosthetics, stop-motion animation, or computer-generated imagery. Out of the pioneers of special effects cinema, it is probably Ray Harryhausen whose monsters have had the most lasting influence on video games. Dubbed "the godfather of both movie monsters and movie special effects," he was the animator behind the skeletons of *Jason and the Argonauts* (1963) and the Kraken and Medusa of *Clash of the Titans* (1981).[19] In a memorable scene from the former, seven stop-motion skeletons rise from the crumbling ground and slowly but surely make their way to Jason and his two comrades (see figure 3.3). A dramatic, spectacularly choreographed fight between the heroes and skeletons ensues; two argonauts are killed and only one skeleton is defeated. Jason retreats to a cliff and escapes the monsters by jumping into the sea.

As the animation scholar Manuel Ferri Gandía has shown, Harryhausen's influence on the monstrous imaginary of video games has been so thorough that video game skeletons tend to equip the same weapon combinations as the ones in the film—and in the 1989 arcade hit *Golden Axe* by Sega, they even rise from the ground in the exact same manner (see figure 3.4).[20] Harryhausen's animation anticipated video game monsters in one more important regard. Rather than creating special effects just for the sake of individual camera takes, he sculpted self-contained miniatures that afforded a complete range of motion needed to animate them. As a result, they could be shot from various angles and re-used in multiple takes, scenes, or even multiple films (one of the seven skeletons fighting Jason had, in fact, already appeared in 1958's *The 7th Voyage of Sinbad*).[21] On several occasions, Harryhausen even

FIGURE 3.3
Ray Harryhausen's skeletons rising and fighting in *Jason and the Argonauts* (1963).

came up with the monster design first and only looked for a story in which to place it later. His approach to special effects, described by film scholar Julie Turnock as "not-too-realistic," foregrounded the work that went into animating monsters, "riveting the viewer through an amazement and appreciation of the artistry and effort of its handcraftedness."[22] His playful,

FIGURE 3.4
Skeletons rising and fighting in the arcade game *Golden Axe* (1989), developed by Sega in Japan.

toy-like creatures were hardly an attempt at sublime monstrosity; instead, they contributed to the proliferation of monster culture, which saw monsters as objects of fan scrutiny and enthusiasm. Despite his deep imprint on popular culture, Harryhausen remained in the margins of the film establishment, not least because the film industry has regarded the work of directing and screenwriting more highly than animation and special effects.

MONSTROUS REALISM

Much like *Jason and the Argonauts* and *Clash of the Titans*, video games have put their monsters front and center—and their reliance on monstrous imagery likely contributed to their reputation as a puerile, culturally marginal, and potentially harmful medium, the "carnivalesque charivari" that conservative critics warned against. But producing video game monsters is not just a matter of capricious experimentation, as the creatures are expected to be believably integrated into the games' simulated environments. In the previous chapter, we saw that the monsters in *D&D* were designed with an eye for "realistic" combat mechanics. I have come across similar concerns in contemporary developer testimonies. The *God of War* reboot team dubbed their aesthetic "mythical realism," while the team behind the 2019 action/role-playing hit *Monster Hunter: World* aimed for "the most realistic creatures yet."[23] How can monsters—which are essentially imaginary creatures—be represented realistically?

Taking inspiration from the subfield of social semiotics, we can understand realism as a set of aesthetic conventions and techniques employed to achieve an acceptable illusion of the real; meaning that there is not just *one* realism, but many different realisms, each situated in a particular historical and cultural context.[24] In the case of monsters, these conventions and techniques tend to be borrowed from representations of nature, especially animals. Viollet-le-Duc once likened gargoyles to prehistoric species, writing that "one thinks to see in these stone bestiaries a lost creation, but proceeding with the logic imposed on all natural creations." To him, creating monsters was a "study of nature applied to a being that does not exist."[25] The art history of monsters attests to a drive for anatomical correctness. Wengrow argues that the creation of the earliest composite creatures required "enhanced accuracy in the depiction of individual body parts, each of which should be rendered at a common scale and should be clearly identifiable."[26] The Renaissance polymath Leonardo da Vinci, who broached the topic in his notebooks, opined that to "make an imaginary animal appear natural," one has to make sure that each body part "bears some resemblance to that of some one of the other animals." A dragon could, in his view, take the head of a mastiff, the eyes of a cat, the temples of an old cock, and the neck of a water-tortoise.[27] Harryhausen has been likewise praised for how rigorously he applied the knowledge of anatomy and biomechanics to his fictitious creatures.[28] The norms of realistic figurative art help the artist give shape to the monstrous and embed it in its habitat, be it the spire of a cathedral or the mise-en-scène of a film. On the other hand, these norms also impose limits on formal experimentation, displacing subjective experiences of otherness with much more stable templates for representing objectivized reality.[29] This is also the case with "realistic" video game monsters.

The audiovisual representation of video game monsters has evolved along with the development of computer graphics and sound. Each alien in *Space Invaders* only consisted of a tiny grid of black or white pixels: zeros or ones. The early 8-bit monsters did in general leave a lot to the imagination. In his poetic homage to Atari 2600 games like *Phoenix* and *Demon Attack*, Mark Lamoureux finds the sublime and the mysterious in the "monsters, strange creatures, demons, and chimeras, all lovingly rendered in blocky bitmaps." Comparing monster graphics to "primitive art," he writes that they employ a style of representation "unburdened by the constraints of realistic mimesis and revels in blocky forms and garish colors."[30] Watching the game on the screen, however, does not tell the whole story. The games' packaging and manuals featured much more detailed and anatomically conventional illustrations of these creatures. *Akalabeth*'s promise of "ten hi-res monsters," as well as the effort that went into drawing the enemies in *dnd*—the mid-1970s adaptation of *D&D*—suggest that players have always savored detail.[31] The abstract shapes and luminescent glow of the early critters might feel mysterious to us today, but for the contemporary audience they were simply the industry standard.

From the mid-1990s onward, most major game productions shifted to 3D graphics, pushing video game artists to think of monsters as sculptures or miniatures, like Viollet-le-Duc and Harryhausen did. The trailblazing 1993 first-person shooter *Doom* rendered environments in 3D, but enemies still as flat sprites. To give their demons more lifelike contours, id Software's artists built them as clay or latex-and-metal models, photographed them from several angles, scanned and colorized the photos, and then imported the images into the game as bitmap data.[32] Since the 2000s, photorealistic 3D graphics for both the game world and its inhabitants have become standard in big-budget titles. Some saw it as untapped potential for monster making. Writing in 2008, Krzywinska compared zombies played by humans with makeup to the 3D zombies of video games, noting that "greater graphical resources" afford artists "greater freedom to construct more fantastical entities" and can lead to "more diverse shapes and forms of zombies."[33] While this is theoretically true, the emphasis on photorealism means that—at least in mainstream big-budget titles—monsters have to be modelled in a high level of detail, commensurable with the surrounding environment. While the dragon does not exist in real life, one still expects it to have lizard scales, and those scales should be rendered with reasonably high fidelity. Although the players are unlikely to ever meet a real-life zombie, they may have high expectations for the physics and visuals of their decaying flesh. This makes production not only more expensive, but also more reliant on the conventions of anatomical plausibility, as I will demonstrate using the case of *God of War*.

BUILDING *GOD OF WAR*'S MONSTERS

Launched in 2005, the original *God of War* trilogy followed the ruthless antihero Kratos and his violent run-ins with the monsters and gods of Greek mythology. David Jaffe, the director of the first game, was heavily influenced by the work of Ray Harryhausen; the designs of Medusa and Kraken are, for example, borrowed almost wholesale from *Clash of the Titans*. There was one important change: breaking from Harryhausen's kid-friendly productions, Jaffe wanted to make the game more brutal. The story of a cynical (demi-)god killing gods and titans embodied the masculine power fantasy that dominated the gaming discourse of the time. When designing combat, Jaffe's team had looked for inspiration in films but realized that "movie fights are really kind of tame when you think about it," hinting at the fact that video game combat is a discipline of its own, which revels in over-the-top scenes of spectacular agency.[34] Doubling down on player vs. environment logic, *God of War* ended up building on the hyperkinetic, hack-and-slash action pioneered by the *Devil May Cry* series (in which a protagonist named Dante fought demons).[35] Its gameplay rhythm depends on large numbers of varied monsters: Kratos does not fight just one minotaur, for example—there are dozens of them to be fought, split into several categories based on their strength, abilities, and moves.

The 2018 installment is both a sequel to and a reboot of the series. Set in a world based on Old Norse mythology, the game's narrative follows an older, timeworn Kratos mourning the death of his wife and coming to grips with fatherhood as he and his son Atreus travel to the highest peak of the world to scatter his wife's ashes. The game has been put forward as an example of *dadification*—a purportedly more mature approach to video game storytelling practiced by and targeted at adult men, which nevertheless reconfirms the masculine power fantasy of defeating enemies while protecting the weak.[36] Along the way, then, Kratos and Atreus kill hundreds of monsters: most frequently Draugar (undead warriors of the Norse legend, *Draugr* in singular), but also Trolls, giants, Valkyries, and others.

Behind-the-scenes materials about the game show that the game's monster design was a result of collaboration across several departments. The creative director Cory Barlog, who had served as the lead animator of the 2005 game and as director of 2007's *God of War II*, set the overall tone, which was supposed to be grittier and more "realistic" than the original trilogy and avoid fantasy clichés.[37] The first steps in the monsters' visual design were taken by concept artists. Their preproduction explorations of the game world tapped into sublime imagery of majestic nature, ancient monuments, and primeval creatures. Much attention was paid to physical detail. The team's principal character artist Rafael Grassetti even created clay maquettes for the protagonists and one prominent monster—a Troll. The miniatures helped the artists communicate a "full sense of the character" to the rest of the team.[38]

Monster design progressed in a series of iterative steps. Although the process was collaborative, the paradoxical requirements of video game monsters created a conceptual tension that was acknowledged and negotiated by the team. The varying concerns of different departments manifest in a short official video about the Trolls. In the clip, Barlog assumes a writer's perspective and outlines their backstory as an ancient population of which only the last handful remain. Grassetti goes on to relate their appearance to their religion, explaining why each of them carries a heavy stone totem that doubles as a weapon. The last to speak is the lead gameplay designer Jason McDonald, who pinpoints the areas on a Troll's body that Kratos can target with his throwing axe and encourages "just getting in there and kicking his ass because Kratos can handle anything."[39] So, while the narrative and art teams give the creature life and history, the gameplay team ensures it can be destroyed—promising that the series' trademark power fantasy is still in place even though the story has been dadified.[40]

For a game to function as a software product, the monsters need to be encoded, and their visual design is therefore shaped by the technical affordances of the game engine and the software tools used in production, such as Autodesk Maya. According to Grassetti, a 2D concept artist has "a clean slate" and is free to come up with "the coolest, craziest stuff" they can think of. There are, however, limits to how these 2D concepts can be translated into 3D models and how they can be animated. If someone designs a creature with "nine tails and three heads and some bat wings," Grassetti explains, it might look great on paper but be difficult to animate. The scale of *God of War*'s monsters was discussed at "scale review" meetings, where artists and animators would push for enemies to be bigger, but gameplay designers—who are in charge of mechanics— wanted them to be smaller because larger creatures are more difficult to implement.[41] True to tradition, though, the finished game does feature towering monsters—the Trolls are so big that Kratos barely reaches their buttocks (see figure 3.5).

FIGURE 3.5
Dauði Kaupmaðr, the first Troll encountered in *God of War* (2018).

For combat designer Denny Yeh, monster design pivots around the question he sums up as: "What can this enemy make the player do?" As Yeh demonstrates using the example of Valkyries, each attack enforces a reaction—in this case, a horizontal throw attack requires blocking, a vertical attack requires dodging sideways, and a ground slam attack can be interrupted by an axe throw or by Atreus's arrow.[42] Attacks are—to use a term from video game jargon—*telegraphed* in advance so that the player has a window of time to react. To that end, a monster should be visible and audible—a user-experience design requirement that may trump artistic and narrative considerations. The majestic earth dragon Hræzlyr, an early boss in the game, was originally envisioned as an albino because he lives inside a mountain. While zoologically plausible, that idea was scrapped because it was difficult to see him against the sky. The animator, Sophie Evans, had originally intended to "raise the claw as high as possible to get a really strong slam down" but realized that then "you lose the claw in this camera view, which really isn't fair for gameplay."[43] Some of the dragon's scale and ferocity that might have been lost in the process is communicated by sound. To create Hræzlyr's roar, the sound designer Daniel Birczyński layered over twenty different sounds, starting with his own manipulated voice and adding animal growls, metallic screeches, and what sounds like chainsaws or helicopters.[44]

The tension between sublime and contained monstrosity that we have observed in the production process also manifests in the game's bestiary. Remediating its ancient and medieval counterparts, it is represented as a leather-bound codex with drawings and descriptions of individual monsters (see figure 3.6). The descriptions are stylized as though written by Atreus. At times, they try to capture the awe and wonder

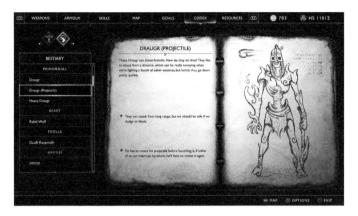

FIGURE 3.6
A bestiary page from *God of War* (2018) showing Draugr (projectile).

that a young boy might feel when encountering mythical monsters. The description of the Stone Ancient, for example, begins: "One of the Ancients . . . I can't believe it! Did Mom know they were still alive? They're, well . . . ancient!" After subsequent encounters, however, the entries are expanded with hints on how to best dispose of these enemies, highlighting their weak spots as well as their status as knowable, defeatable entities. Moreover, the naming and taxonomy of the monsters in the bestiary follow the classification of their mechanical behavior. Draugar come in several gameplay varieties: Draugr (projectile), Draugr (power weapon), Draugr (speed), or Draugr (shield). These parenthesized code names—traces of the game's database structure—inhabit the pages of the virtual codex, creating an awkward combination of medieval and contemporary contained monstrosity.

While typical of mainstream, big-budget titles, not all productions follow the same workflow as *God of War*. The team behind *Monster Hunter: World* went even further in their effort to "realistically" depict monsters as "lost creations" indigenous to the game's fictional world.[45] In this case, monster designers worked in tandem with level designers to create simulated eco-systems of creatures that interact quasi-realistically with each other and their environment. The dinosaur-like beast Great Jagras, for example, "balloons in size after a big meal" and the body of the elder dragon Nergigante is covered by more than a thousand thorns, each of which "exists completely indepen-dently on its body" and may individually regenerate.[46] But make no mistake—although many of the game's missions are assigned by a character called "chief ecologist" and carried out in the name of "research," the goal is usually to kill the crea-tures and haul their carcasses to the base.

For games that do not belong to an ongoing franchise with a well-established fictional world, the monster design process might be reversed: monsters may be designed mechanically first and only later receive a visual representation and a sonic signature. This was the case with Splicers, the basic monsters of the acclaimed first-person shooter *BioShock*.[47] Originally envisioned as bulky, B-movie mutants, they became much more human-like when the team decided to make them more relatable.[48] And while it might be hard to imagine *Plants vs. Zombies* without zombies, this tower defense hit game was initially envisioned with aliens in mind.[49]

To develop the point made by Rafael Grassetti, the produc-tion pipeline of 3D animation constrains the range of shapes that can be conveniently and affordably animated. When making a 3D game on a tighter budget, studios might choose human-proportioned creatures (like zombies) over oddly shaped monsters, because the former can be adapted from the already available human 3D models (*meshes*) and templates for skeletal animations (*rigs*). Developer interviews attest to the fact that "zombies are a cheap animation expense because they use a 'human rig' and usually only have melee attacks."[50] Olof Strand, the 3D artist working on *Amnesia: The Dark Descent*, explains that he derived the game's monsters from a human model because "using already existing meshes as a starting point is, when possible, very important for production efficiency."[51] (Unsurprisingly, the "human model" in question is a male human model of standard build.) With the emergence of so-called *asset stores*, it is now even possible to purchase ready-made animated monsters for standard game engines. For example, the "Skeleton Lightweight" for the Unreal Engine—a spitting image of Harryhausen's from *Jason and the Argonauts*—can be bought for just twenty dollars.[52] The reasons for the popularity of zombies, Draugar, and other slightly deformed humans are therefore not only cultural or aesthetic but also related to production routines and technical affordances.

BOSS ENCOUNTERS

Boss monsters can be considered the pinnacle of video game monster design. They are bigger, more challenging, and more spectacular than regular monsters; they offer climactic conclusions to games or their sections and structure the gameplay experience. The first video game boss monster—a dragon—reportedly appeared already in *dnd* in the mid-1970s.[53] In the arcade space, boss monsters date back to 1980's *Phoenix*, which spiced up the *Space Invaders* formula by adding a separate stage with an octopus hiding inside a gigantic mothership.[54] The 1983 shoot-em-up *Xevious* has been credited with solidifying the practice by unleashing its boss at the end of each level.[55] Thanks to their inclusion in hits like *Super Mario Bros.* (featuring Bowser) and *The Legend of Zelda* (featuring the boar-like Ganon), bosses have become something of a norm in player vs. environment games.[56] In a short but poignant thought piece on the topic, technology writer Clive Thompson celebrates boss battles as "the most mythopoeic part of gaming."[57] They aim to instill fear and awe and offer a glimpse of sublime monstrosity.

A good example of a boss may be *Bloodborne*'s Cleric Beast, the first major enemy you are likely to come across in this game (see figure 3.7). As your character tries to cross a bridge between two parts of a nightmare Gothic city, a huge yet gaunt abomination screeches, jumps over a wall, and runs toward your avatar. The first thing you notice is its *scale*. As it ominously limps and jumps toward you, you realize you can barely reach its knees—bosses often dwarf both the

FIGURE 3.7
Fighting the Cleric Beast in *Bloodborne* (2015).

protagonist and regular enemies, despite the technical challenges this brings. Secondly, it is a *unique* enemy. This means both that it is not fungible in the sense discussed in the previous chapter and that it is qualitatively different. Until now, you have mostly battled human hunters and rabid dogs, but Cleric Beast is something else. Clearly a monstrous fusion, it has some vaguely humanoid features as well as horns and wolf-like claws. The unkempt hair on its back flutters in the air, gracefully demonstrating the capabilities of then-contemporary graphics hardware. It has a unique moveset, too. The game's creative director Hidetaka Miyazaki, who has been closely involved in the boss design of his titles, points out the "unique idiosyncrasies" of each.[58] One strange thing about the Cleric Beast is that it is asymmetrical—it has a huge left arm capable of powerful grabs. Third, bosses also tend to have an important place within a game's *thematic* and narrative structure. According to Miyazaki, Cleric Beast is designed to epitomize the deeper conflict between humanity and bestiality—referring to the in-game legend that members of the church (clerics) turned into the fiercest beasts because they so resisted the urge to go beastly that it was building up inside them.[59]

The fourth—and perhaps the most important—feature of bosses is *difficulty*. In a quote for Thompson's article, Ian Bogost opines that "really good bosses seem impossible at first."[60] This aligns with Asma's observation that sublime monstrosity evokes the feeling of "radical vulnerability" because of the "uneven and unfair power proportions" between the monster and the protagonist.[61] For a newcomer to *Bloodborne*, Cleric Beast may be frustratingly tough. If the protagonist dawdles in front of it, it can easily grab them with its left hand and wipe out most of their health bar. It is difficult to avoid the Beast's hits as the battle takes place on a narrow bridge, and it is easy to get cornered. To add insult to injury, the boss gets progressively stronger. At a certain point, the Beast shrouds itself in red vapor and gains a new, even fiercer set of moves, which steps up the difficulty just as the player believes that victory is within reach. Called a "heat-up system" by Miyazaki, such phase-like structure—which may follow a boss's various metamorphoses—is common in the design of bosses, as opposed to ordinary monsters, whose behavior tends to be uniform throughout the fight.[62]

In the end, though, boss battles are designed to be won by the player. According to a rare user study of boss fight reception, "fairness" is considered even more important than "challenge" in making for an enjoyable battle.[63] Writing of the Valkyries he designed for *God of War*, Denny Yeh indeed stresses that bosses have to be challenging but fair: "Every single thing the Valkyrie can do has an answer. Every time you die against a Valkyrie, you know there was something you could have done differently to prevent it," adding that "when a Valkyrie tries to step on your face or chop off your head with a scythe, she's really just saying 'I value your education.'"[64] Boss fights are puzzles of sorts and usually require observation and practice. To quote Bogost via Thompson, bosses "provide incremental clues to weaken them."[65] It might take a few defeats to find out that the Cleric Beast's moveset—which might seem inscrutable at first—can be divided into four basic attacks, each of which can be avoided. The Beast's physiognomy gives an additional important clue:

it is advisable to keep to the left to face the monster's weaker hand and avoid its powerful grabs. The "education" needed here includes not only the time spent tackling the specific boss and internalizing its moves but also the knowledge of general game design conventions and—in games with action-based combat like *Bloodborne*—the required motor skills.[66] Tough bosses are a boon to the makers of metatextual materials such as strategy guides and walkthrough videos, where all the bosses of *Bloodborne* have been dissected with zoological precision, effectively containing their sublime qualities.

The delicate balancing act between challenge and fairness makes boss fights a showcase for "game design at its purest and trickiest."[67] As a result, they tend to be situated in enclosed arenas so that the range of possible interactions is limited. Such is also the case with the Cleric Beast—impenetrable fog blocks all the exits from the bridge, which means one cannot lure it into more advantageous terrain. As boss fights are often separate and tightly choreographed, I have previously likened them to song-and-dance numbers in Bollywood films.[68] In fact, some have been criticized for being inconsistent with the rest of the game. The infamous boss battles of *Deus Ex: Human Revolution* were outsourced to a different studio because of time constraints. The battles required much more action-oriented gameplay than the rest of the game, which allowed for a nonlethal stealthy approach. The head of the outsourcing studio did admit that balancing the difficulty was "brutally hard."[69] Besides demonstrating the complexity of video game production, the story also testifies to the urge to include bosses even if they jar with games' basic mechanics and threaten production deadlines.

Despite—or perhaps because of—their omnipresence, not everyone is happy about bosses. Veteran shoot-'em-up game designer Jeff Minter bemoans boss battles as an excuse for stereotypical design:

> Older shooters, although arguably more primitive, were often more creative in terms of controls and enemy behaviours than before everything became a series of reworkings of *Xevious*. [My games are] almost an attempt to imagine how such games might have evolved if their evolution hadn't been stunted by endless versions of *Xevious* and bosses.[70]

In his view, the challenge and spectacle provided by the bosses are used to Band-Aid over otherwise simple and repetitive mechanics. From a production budget perspective, bosses consume significant resources and creative effort in exchange for a climactic but relatively small chunk of the game. At the same time, the level of challenge in boss fights, while welcomed by hard-core gamers, might be off-putting to less proficient players. In recent years, several major titles have opted to make many or all boss fights optional. Discussing *God of War*, designer Denny Yeh has placed boss fights on a scale from "spectacle bosses" to "combat bosses."[71] The former include the mandatory but relatively easy fight against Hræzlyr; they are heavily cinematic and were apparently costly to make. On the combat side of the spectrum are the challenging but optional fights against Valkyries; these are comparatively modest in terms of production values and intended mostly as tests of skill for advanced players. 2019's paranormal-themed shooter *Control* went even further as all of its traditional boss fights occur in optional (sometimes even hidden) side missions.

HUMAN TOUCH

I have likened video game monsters to daemons that execute the agency of the machine. To control them, most commercial games tend to employ rule-based techniques like finite state machines or behavior trees, which execute scripted reactions to predefined sets of conditions.[72] A Troll in *God of War* will, for instance, quite predictably use different attacks depending on his distance from Kratos. The algorithms that drive monsters have become more complex over the years, but commercial games are nowhere near widely implementing artificial intelligence (AI) that would learn from the player's actions—in part because designers would have to cede control over player experience.[73]

Although video game monsters do not possess human-like intelligence, they bear the imprints of their designers and include elements of human performance. David W. Bradley, the game designer renowned for his work on the *Wizardry* computer RPG series, was once asked what kind of character he would create to play through its latest installment. He replied: "Well, actually, I am in [the game], but I'm all of the other creatures in the game."[74] Before writing computer games, Bradley had been an avid tabletop role-player and must have learned that a dungeon master not only conducts or designs an adventure but also *performs* as nonplayer characters and monsters.

When speaking of his adventure films, Harryhausen attributed his ability to create expressive and memorable creatures to his acting training. He felt that he could "act" through his models while animating them and thus make them feel less artificial.[75] Game designers also strive to overcome the impression of mechanical artifice—unless they are creating robot monsters. This effort can be illustrated by the example of the 2009 hack-and-slash title *Bayonetta*, celebrated for its elegant, high-speed combat. The game pits the titular witch against an army of corrupted angels, which boast some of the most distinctive and opulent audiovisual monster designs within the genre (see figure 3.8). Conceived primarily by the enemy artist Yusuke Hashimoto, they invoke the morphological experimentation of marginal monstrosity and have been described as "complicated amalgamations of marble, gold and velvet, as if chunks of Saint Peter's Basilica had suddenly come to life."[76] But the game owes its success just as much to the programmer Kazunori Inoue and his feel for enemy movement. In a summary of his monster design tips, Inoue details his method of putting himself in the monster's shoes:

FIGURE 3.8
Iustitia, one of the boss enemies in *Bayonetta* (2009). According to the game's bestiary, Iustitia "is known to take a particularly strange physical manifestation" and "could easily pass for a demon."

> I tend to get cold towards things that make me feel like I
> am fighting against a computer. When I make an enemy,
> I treat it as an extension of myself, so if I feel that I myself
> couldn't react and dodge in a certain amount of time, I
> am not going to allow an enemy to do that either. Nor
> will I ever let an enemy do some sort of attack that can't
> be dodged even though the player is reacting to it.[77]

Inoue advises designers to avoid simple patterns that allow
the player to easily create strategies to beat their foes. During
the design process, he tries to put monsters on the screen as
soon as possible and stealthily watches his colleagues play.
If they get stuck in the groove with just one go-to move, he
secretly works up a "counter to their addiction."[78] His reactions and observations therefore become a part of the monsters' encoded mechanics.

With the growing demands for graphic fidelity, big-budget
game development has largely moved to using motion capture (mo-cap) for character animation. This not only contributes to more life-like animation of human characters but
also makes the process more efficient, as animating by hand
with the level of detail expected in contemporary blockbusters is extremely time-consuming. *God of War*, for example,
reportedly contains roughly 80 percent mo-cap animation—
including, for example, some moves of the Draugar.[79] In addition, facial-expression data captured with human actors was
applied to some nonhuman creatures, including the gigantic
serpent Jörmungandr.[80] Not only human characters but also
monsters can thus be performed by human actors and stunt
performers.

A striking, well-documented example comes from the
2020 action adventure *The Last of Us Part II*, which features

zombie-like monsters overtaken by fungal infection. The game's only traditional boss monster is the Rat King, an abhorrent fusion of multiple humans connected by fungal growth. When designing it, lead animator Jeremy Yates found inspiration in the movements of conjoined twins, an existing anatomical anomaly. The mo-cap for the Rat King was performed by three stunt actors tied to each other; all three had to be "incredibly strong and have a lot of endurance."[81] Production of video game monsters can therefore rely on demanding physical labor. This practice is not limited to vaguely human-like creatures, as even some reptile animations in *Monster Hunter: World* were performed by human actors.[82] In all of these cases, mo-cap data is, of course, processed and manipulated, but the acting performance remains an inseparable part of the in-game creature. Contrary to Krzywinska's 2008 prediction, the development of more advanced graphics did not fully replace the "man in the suit;" instead, it has replaced the latex suit with a mo-cap suit.[83]

Monster design, then, often requires humans to assume the perspective of the enemy and become the model for its appearance or behavior. As a practice that includes elements of acting and puppetry, it endows the creatures with the performances and sensibilities of actors and designers. Like the behind-the-scenes scoops from the *Famous Monsters of Filmland* magazine in the 1960s, video footage of humans performing as monsters highlight the creative and physical labor involved in the process. These materials complicate the demarcation between humans and monsters (which will be discussed in the next chapter), and they also chip away at the sublime mystery of these man-made creatures.

Whereas the previous chapter examined the player vs. environment model as a conceptual foundation for video game monstrosity, this chapter has explored how this model is brought to life in contemporary game development. Unlike their medieval counterparts, video game monsters are not marginal to the main body of work; they are central to the game experience and stand ready to become objects of not only our gaze but also our actions. To return to the example of silhouette tests: Monsters should be not only visually impressive but also easily distinguishable and identifiable as targets of interaction. They telegraph their attacks and reveal their weak spots to guide player action. Their design is ultimately guided by the concern for a satisfying user experience and entertaining game mechanics.

Besides the rules of player vs. environment engagement, this chapter has identified three major factors that affect how a monster will look and sound in a video game: first, the set of norms and conventions of audiovisual monster representation inherited from other media and domains of art, including manuscript illumination, ecclesiastical sculpture, film, and—although I did not discuss it directly—comics. The second factor is the technology used for creating and executing the game: the 3D modelling software, rendering engines, and other tools. In other words, a monster is made to fit the studio's production pipeline. Returning to some examples of sublime monstrosity from the first chapter, one may guess that if the Babylonian monster god Marduk had appeared in *God of War*, his "outstanding form" would have been rendered as about five to ten times the height of Kratos, depending on the severity of scale review. The third important factor in monster design is the creative work of artists, designers, and actors. The analysis in this chapter is meant as a testament to the creativity needed to negotiate the paradoxical requirements of video game monstrosity and to "create and combine"—as Camille put it—existing forms into new ones.

Together, chapters 2 and 3 have described the baseline for much of today's video game monstrosity. While monster theory highlights the sublime and incomprehensible nature of the monster, video games tend to present monsters as contained, objectified, and manageable—by the player, by the computer hardware, and by the production processes. The final chapter will explore the monsters that subvert the conventions of the player vs. environment model and offer fresh new takes on enemy design.

4

NEW HAUNTS

It seems evil, but it's just with the wrong crowd . . .

—In-game description of Migosp, a monster in *Undertale*[1]

How far have video game monsters come since *Space Invaders* and *Gauntlet*? Today's zombies shamble more realistically, the giants are even more gigantic, and the dragons have their scales rendered in such detail that one is tempted to touch them. Games like *Bayonetta* and *Bloodborne* have given us intricate bosses and beautifully twisted audiovisual designs. Conceptually, though, very little has changed. Killing monsters to progress, one after another, has remained a rarely contested paradigm in action and role-playing video game design since the late 1970s. Thanks to the creative efforts of game designers and audiovisual artists, it remains popular and entertaining. But as recounted earlier in this book, the player vs. environment formula is very much of its time. It presupposes—like Cold War–era military models did—that hostile others can be easily recognized and predicted; it reflects the neoliberal emphasis on individual struggle and personal growth by creating a satisfying but distracting flow state. It comforts us, suggesting that all our adversaries can be beaten.

In the world around us, however, much has changed since the 1970s. The subsequent decades have brought about new threats that are distributed and pervasive: pandemics, global extremism and terrorism, unchecked corporate greed, and, most importantly, climate change. The environmental crises facing mankind have shattered the notion of a human subject that can be extricated from the world they inhabit. The possibility of creating closed worlds insulated from outside threat has likewise proven illusory. In the Anthropocene—a geological epoch defined by human impact—we are threatened by monsters of our own making.[2] As Bruno Latour notes of a tornado: "We are no longer watching the tornado from a safe haven as if in no way responsible for its occurrence."[3] In his view, this spells the end of the traditional notion of a natural sublime that relied on the contrast between the forces of nature and the certainty that the human mind was capable of overcoming them. I would argue, however, that the notion of sublime monstrosity in the sense of unfathomable, awe-inspiring otherness is still valid—although it has become a painfully immediate result of human action.

Discourses about otherness have also evolved. Gender studies, postcolonial scholarship, and animal studies have all revealed the extent to which otherness is socially constructed rather than "natural."[4] Incorporating these developments into monster theory, Patricia MacCormack proposes a *posthuman teratology* that questions not only the concept of monstrosity but also that of humanity:

> The posthuman challenges not only qualities which make
> up the human—as an organism and a cultural, reflective,

knowing subject (including knowledge of self)—but qualities which compel the paradigms by which things are perceived to be able to be known. These include organism or
object discretion, the possibility of essence, the promise of
investigation being exhausted when the object is known
absolutely, belief in the myth of objectivity or the possibility of the observer being entirely extricated from the
observed . . . [5]

Monster culture has reflected these shifts. According to
cultural scholar Jeffrey Andrew Weinstock, one important
change in the Western understanding of the monster was the
"disconnection of monstrosity from physical appearance,"
initiated by the Romantics and further popularized in the
twentieth century. As Mary Shelley's *Frankenstein*—an early
example of this decoupling—shows, looking monstrous no
longer implies being evil or immoral. The recent retellings of
Beowulf, a classic monster-slaying epic, are also sympathetic
to the monster's perspective; John Gardner's 1971 novel *Grendel* is written from the point of view of the monster, and the
2007 Robert Zemeckis film likewise portrays him as a misunderstood outcast. Weinstock argues that as a result of this
shift, monstrosity is "reconfigured as a kind of invisible disease that eats away at the body politic, and manifests visibly
through symptomatic behavior."[6] He suggests four manifestations of this new, invisible monstrosity: (1) the figure
of the psychopath who cannot be, at first sight, told apart
from ordinary people; (2) the faceless and tentacular corporation that thrives on greed and corruption; (3) the virus that
destroys the body and disrupts the functioning of society; and
(4) the nature that responds to its destruction at the hands
of humans.[7] To Weinstock's list, we might add (5) advanced

computer technology that threatens to escape human control, notably embodied in hostile sentient networks such as the Skynet from the *Terminator* franchise. As Linne Henriksen and coauthors have pointed out, "technological developments, the supposed antithesis to the realm of monsters and the supernatural, have attributed to making the world more monstrous and 'haunted.' "[8]

The age of discrete and well-defined monsters seems long past. Roger Luckhurst, expanding on previous work by Steffen Hantke, suggests that most twenty-first-century monster movies misfire "because the singular, irruptive, invasive monster is badly adapted to the 'times of perpetual emergency.' " He adds that "Godzilla and his progeny are fatally tied to a prior epoch of punctual nuclear or invasion threats, and after 9/11 they fall out of sync with the times."[9] Godzilla—as well as the monster of *Cloverfield* (2008)—represents a localized threat that is enormous but, at least in theory, destructible by concentrated military firepower.[10] To highlight a new approach to monstrosity in mainstream film, Luckhurst points to Gareth Edwards' 2010 film *Monsters*.[11] The film's tentacular monsters, which inhabit an expansive border territory between the United States and Mexico, remain hidden for most of the film. When the protagonists finally glimpse two of these gigantic monsters in a final climactic sequence, the latter do not attack; instead, they seem "indifferent to the human dynamics taking place below them."[12] To Luckhurst, it is futile to look for the monsters' hidden meanings; they are not a metaphor for anything—they just *are*. Overall, both the current crises and the intellectual responses to them have destabilized the privileged vantage point of an observer who can identify and interpret a given being as a monstrous other.

AGAINST THE ONTOLOGY OF THE ENEMY

Video games have responded to the new threats and new approaches to monstrosity, but they very often do so solely on the thematic level: the *Resident Evil* series features the Umbrella Corporation as a larger-than-life, evil force animating its plots, while *The Last of Us* series (like many others) is set in a world decimated by a pandemic. These larger threats are, however, made to fit the player vs. environment paradigm by dissolving them into groups of well-defined enemies, most commonly zombies. Does it mean that video games, like traditional monster movies, are "out of sync with the times"?

To answer this question, we must revisit the foundations of the player vs. environment mode of play. Most video game combat follows the principles of the ontology of the enemy, the Cold War–era approach to otherness that sees anything that moves as a hostile, calculable target.[13] Contemporary posthuman monstrosity, however, contradicts this ontology in two important ways. First, the Cold War–era doctrine assumes that a hostile enemy is discernible from the subject (or "us") and its allies. But as Weinstock has pointed out, monstrosity is already here with us, in our body politic (like the psychopaths or corporations Weinstock mentions) or even in our physical bodies (like the virus). In fact, it is *we* who are monsters to each other, to other species and to nature more broadly. This first contradiction can be called a *failure of distancing*, as the subject cannot tell itself from the monster; the hero becomes monstrous while the monsters become sympathetic. Second, the ontology of the enemy presupposes that a hostile being is within reach of calculation and targeting. But contemporary threats cannot be destroyed by conventional weaponry.

Posthuman monstrosity may be so elusive, complex, or indifferent that it avoids scrutiny and confrontation. We can call this contradiction a *failure of engagement*, as the subject is unable to engage the monster.

Both contradictions have been already acknowledged throughout the history of video games, for various reasons and with various intentions. The failure of distancing notably manifests in the trope of the monstrous double, or a doppelgänger. Perhaps its most influential video game example comes from the 1989 Apple II game *Prince of Persia* by Jordan Mechner.[14] Originally, the game was designed with no combat at all, and Mechner was reluctant to add enemies because he had already run out of the Apple II's limited memory. At the insistence of his office mate, he engineered an adversary by simply shifting the color bits of the main character's animation frames.[15] The resulting ghostly figure—whom Mechner and friends immediately nicknamed Shadow Man—appears after the protagonist jumps into a magic mirror, becoming his nemesis and hampering his progress at pre-scripted points. Close to the end of the game, the player may finally engage the Shadow Man in a swordfight (see figure 4.1). By that point, the player has defeated numerous other enemies (including skeletons) that Mechner ended up squeezing into the code. However, any damage dealt to Shadow Man is also felt by the prince, underscoring their unbreakable connection. The only solution is to sheath the sword, walk into the Shadow Man, and merge with him. Although initially motivated by technological constraints, this encounter is a narrative and conceptual highlight of the whole title. Since then, monstrous doubles have appeared in numerous games, often

FIGURE 4.1
The battle against Shadow Man in *Prince of Persia* (1989).

designed to let the player experience the same treatment they give to the enemies.[16]

A memorable example of the failure of engagement comes from the 1977 text adventure *Zork*, written by a team of MIT students who later formed the company Infocom. Inspired by the settings and narratives of *D&D*, the text-only game features several classic fantasy monsters that can be out-smarted by figuring out puzzle-like solutions. There is, how-ever, another, far more original creature—the Grue. It came about as a game design measure to prevent players from mov-ing around dark areas without a light source. In the original game, the player is warned of the lurking Grue by the sin-ister message: "It is pitch black. You are likely to be eaten by a grue." If the warning goes unheeded, the game reports that "a fearsome grue slithered into the room and devoured you."[17] The game offers no means of examining or defeating the Grue—the monster is a pure expression of the programmers' will to limit player behavior. Its mysterious nature captured the imagination of the computer gaming community and has been called "one of the very first great original monsters of the computer age."[18] While subsequent Infocom games fleshed out the details, it was the original that helped Grue become a household name.[19]

In the rest of this chapter, I focus on further contemporary examples of such subversions. My goal is not to provide an exhaustive list of unconventional video game monsters but rather to sketch out a set of major trajectories in the design of subversive monstrous adversaries. First, I focus on games that exemplify the failure of distancing—titles that question the heroism of the protagonist and the monstrosity of the enemies. Then, I move on to games that present failures of engagement—monsters that are invisible or inscrutable, monsters that are deindividuated and uncountable, and, finally, monsters that take over the game's code and interface.

THE MELANCHOLY OF A MONSTER KILLER

One way of challenging traditional monster narratives is by casting doubt on the heroism of the monster slayer. In the Western tradition, this line of thinking far precedes the Anthropocene and can be identified in early Christianity. One of its most famous formulations appeared in the essay "Beowulf: The Monsters and the Critics" by J. R. R. Tolkien. Tolkien argues that monsters are critical to understanding the poem's poetic qualities. In his view, they provide a perspective that "surpasses the dates and limits of historical periods"—in other words, they evoke a feeling of the sublime.[20] At the same time, he makes it clear that killing monsters should not be understood as inherently virtuous. He sides with the poet of Beowulf in rejecting the notion of "martial heroism as its own end."[21] Despite his ever more difficult exploits, the proud warrior Beowulf faces the "tragedy of inevitable ruin" that no earthly fame or fortune can prevent.[22] Although he kills the dragon—the poem's final "boss"—he is mortally wounded and dies soon afterward. Tolkien's approach to Beowulf's heroism stems from his Catholic faith, which informed both his academic and fiction work. As summarized by Asma, Tolkien adopts the early Christian view that "without Christianity, monster killers are either hopeless existential heroes, trying by pathetic human effort to rid the world of evil, or they are themselves monstrous giants amid a flock of righteous and meek devotees."[23] Accordingly, Tolkien reads Beowulf as a tragic hero, concluding that the poem is an elegy rather than an epic.[24]

Tragically portrayed monster killers are not uncommon. As pointed out by Krzywinska, the theme of a "false hero," handed down from Gothic literature and film, is typical of horror and fantasy video games.[25] The somber, elegiac tone colors many titles that employ the player vs. environment model while simultaneously questioning it. A prime example of such a game is *Shadow of the Colossus*, widely acknowledged as a milestone in enemy design and ethical gameplay.[26] Its story follows a young man named Wander who travels into a forbidden land to bring his dead lover back to life. An unseen, mysterious entity tells Wander that in exchange, he must slay sixteen colossi—gigantic creatures that inhabit various corners of the land (see figure 4.2). To defeat them, Wander must identify and reach one or more of their weak points (or "vitals"). Unsurprisingly for an action-adventure game, each colossus poses a unique puzzle, inspired by the bosses of the *Legend of Zelda* series. *Shadow of the Colossus*, however, departs from the formula in at least three aspects.

First, there are no mobs in the game. The reasoning behind this decision was both practical and artistic. As the game's producer Kenji Kaido said in an interview, they did it "so the team's resources could be concentrated on the [colossi]," but also to underline the "contrast between the quietness of travelling and the fighting."[27] As a result, the game offers no easy satisfaction of hacking and slashing through weaker opponents. Second, Wander can—and often must—scale, balance on, and hold onto the monsters, often by grabbing onto their fur. As Kaido pointed out, "they are part building, and part living creatures."[28] A colossus is not merely an opponent

FIGURE 4.2
Wander encountering the third colossus. Screenshot from the 2018 remake of *Shadow of the Colossus*.

the protagonist fights, but it is also the ground on which he stands. When the colossi try to shake him off, Wander becomes quite literally an unstable subject—he spends long minutes pressed against the monsters, temporarily merging with their body mass before stabbing them with his magic sword (see figure 4.3). Finally, the destruction of colossi is framed as ethically questionable. In a retrospective interview, the game's director Fumito Ueda reminisced that throughout the production of the game, he "started having doubts about simply 'feeling good by beating monsters' and 'getting sense of accomplishment.'"[29] The colossi are largely peaceful until Wander attacks them. Although the player may experience triumph when beating them (and, in the 2018 remake, collect PlayStation trophies for each), the game's audiovisual design suggests the exact opposite. When stabbed by Wander's sword, they roar and writhe in pain as black blood sprays from their wounds, and their eventual demise is accompanied by melancholy music.[30] To illustrate how unusual this was at the time, Ueda recounted that when he first showed the music to his staff, "they thought it was a bug and laughed because they were so used to games that would play a fanfare after defeating a monster."[31]

From the outset, Wander's nightmarish quest is portrayed as futile and senseless. The Japanologist Miguel César situates the game's narrative in a longer history of representations of what he calls "essential boundary transgressions" between life and death in Japanese folk and popular culture. In his view, "all its mechanics, the design choices and narrative work in that direction: to convince the players of how wrong and dangerous the [transgression] is, even if the game is forcing them to do it."[32] Wander's boundary transgression

FIGURE 4.3
Wander stabbing the third colossus while holding onto it in the 2018
remake of *Shadow of the Colossus*.

is shown as an "immoral selfish act," but the player has no
choice but to push on and witness Wander's inevitable ruin.[33]

While *Shadow of the Colossus* is deeply rooted in Japanese
rather than Western Christian culture, it aligns with Tolkien's
observation about the inherent tragedy of monster killers
whose motivations are selfish rather than morally just.[34] It
also sends an environmental message, casting doubt on the
need to tame and neutralize the forces of nature, represented
by the colossi. *Shadow of the Colossus*, of course, is not the only
game to question the conduct of the monster killer. *Bloodborne*
and *Dark Souls* (whose spectacular monsters are likely inspired
by the colossi) also present fighting monsters as a dreadful,
melancholy affair, equally tragic for everyone involved. In a
telling anecdote, these games' director Hidetaka Miyazaki—
well known for creating "sad" monsters—asked a concept
artist to redo a gross-out design for an undead dragon with

the instruction: "Can't you instead try to convey the deep sorrow of a magnificent beast doomed to a slow and possibly endless descent into ruin?"[35] All three games suggest that the plight of the monster killer is inseparable from the plight of the monsters, an observation famously summed up in Friedrich Nietzsche's aphorism: "Whoever fights with monsters should see to it that he does not become one himself. And when you stare for a long time into an abyss, the abyss stares back into you."[36] This realization resonates with the experience of learning the monsters' mechanics to defeat them, which is common to many player vs. environment video games. As Denny Yeh has noted about monster design for *God of War*, designing an enemy also means designing what it can "make the player do." If enemy moves are designed as complementary to the ones of the protagonist, then the hero is inevitably tainted with the monstrosity of their foes.

The "false hero" theme and the distrust in what the game asks us to do has become a common element in mainstream game storytelling, concurrent with the dadification trend mentioned in the previous chapter. Titles such as *BioShock* or *Spec Ops: The Line* contain plot twists that likewise reveal the protagonist has committed abhorrent deeds and that the player is complicit.[37] Even the dadified reboot of *God of War*, discussed at length in the previous chapter, preempts the question of whether one must kill humanoid monsters. Before the encounter with the first Troll, the dumbfounded Atreus asks: "We're going to fight that?!?," and Kratos answers: "We have no choice," in a matter-of-fact, almost resigned way, as if shruggingly accepting the design conventions of player vs. environment gameplay.[38]

SYMPATHY FOR THE MONSTER

While *Shadow of the Colossus* is a somber game with a desaturated color palette and wistful music, the player vs. environment model can just as well be subverted by humor and parody. Few games have reframed the role of monsters as comprehensively as 2015's *Undertale*, in many ways an homage to parodic JRPGs such as the *Mother* series.[39] Written almost single-handedly by the debuting US developer Toby Fox, it soon became one of the most beloved indie games of its time. Its story follows a child protagonist who falls down a hole into monster-inhabited underground ruins and looks for a way back to the surface. The game follows *D&D* conventions like random encounters, hit points, experience points (EXP), and character levels (LV, alternatively spelled as LOVE), while the combat mechanics owe inspiration to *Space Invaders* and its descendants, featuring "bullet hell" sequences in which the player must avoid myriads of enemy projectiles. Unlike early *D&D* and *Space Invaders*, however, *Undertale* portrays monsters as deserving of empathy. As Fox himself put it in an interview:

> I feel that it's important to make every monster feel like an individual. If you think about it basically all monsters in RPGs like *Final Fantasy* are the same, save for the graphics. They attack you, you heal, you attack them, they die. There's no meaning to that.[40]

The inhabitants of the underground are all called "monsters," and meeting many of them will bring up a familiar-looking combat interface. However, when "checking" monsters using a designated command, or just by observing their behavior, one finds out that they have quirks and concerns that are

not monstrous at all. Of a frog named Froggit—perhaps the
weakest foe in the game—we can read that "life is difficult for
this enemy." A monster called Snowdrake is not only a drake
(male duck) shaped like a snowflake but also an aspiring teen
comedian with many bad puns up his sleeve. It is difficult to
distance oneself from these creatures and treat them as just
enemies (see figure 4.4).

The game's encounter system was inspired by the JRPG
series *Shin Megami Tensei*, which has allowed the protagonist
to negotiate with demons since its first installment in 1992.[41]
Undertale's monsters can be defeated in combat—by dealing
damage and surviving the bullet hell sequences—but other
actions are also available, allowing for sparing the monsters

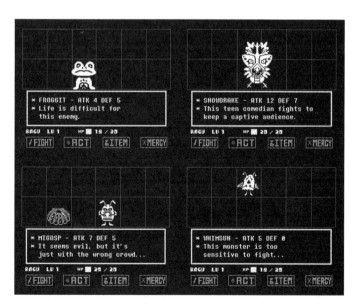

FIGURE 4.4
A montage of four monster encounters in *Undertale* (2015).

instead of killing them. To spare Snowdrake, for example, one must either laugh at his puns or repeatedly heckle him. When it comes to bosses, sparing them entails solving elaborate puzzles. A peaceful resolution of the encounter with Dogi, a pair of canine guards enamored of each other, requires rolling around in the dirt so that the protagonist smells like a "weird puppy," and then petting both of them. The Dogi respond by saying: "Dogs can pet other dogs??? (A new world has opened up for us . . .) Thanks, weird puppy!"

Such a wide range of contextual interactions is made possible by the game's sparse approach to visual representation. Most monsters are shown as simple, black-and-white bitmaps and the interactions are mostly described in text. By avoiding the dictate of photorealism, the game can grant its monsters strange, elusive qualities, which might not be sublime but can be easily read as *queer*—both in the sense of strangeness and of nonnormative gender identity. Accordingly, Bo Ruberg views *Undertale* as a queer video game that shows "a genuine fascination with questioning and . . . queering bodies," pointing out that many characters (including the protagonist) have indeterminate gender identities or "express queer romantic interests."[42] In many other games, encounters with monstrosity inevitably lead to death and destruction. In *Undertale*, the hero can experiment with a range of nonviolent interactions and probe their own identity.

The fact that killing in *Undertale* is avoidable does not mean that the game lacks a villain. In *Shadow of the Colossus*, the true antagonist is the entity that tasks Wander with killing colossi. In *Undertale*, the role of the deceitful guide belongs to Flowey the Flower. At the beginning, Flowey offers a tutorial of the battle mechanics and asserts his belief that "in this world, it's kill or be killed"—a clear expression of the player vs. environment formula. Contrary to Flowey's advice, the game can be finished without a single kill, leading to a special ending, but this pacifist route is markedly more difficult. Although the player must still avoid the monsters' attacks, sparing them earns no EXP, and the protagonist therefore gains neither LV/LOVE nor additional hit points. This makes the player character increasingly vulnerable as the game progresses. Given the difficulty of the game, it is understandable that the player would resort to killing at least some monsters to gain EXP and LV/LOVE. Right before the end, however, one of the recurring non-player characters reveals the lie at the heart of these mechanics: EXP actually stands for "extermination points" and LV/LOVE for "level of violence." This twist is not just a subversion of Flowey's sinister advice but of player vs. environment game design conventions at large. True malice resides not in the monsters themselves but in the way they are classified as enemies and sacrificed at the altar of increasing stats.

Undertale is far from the only game that humanizes its monsters. One of the first games to portray some of its monsters as sympathetic was 1990's *Ultima VI: The False Prophet*, whose plot revolved around the discovery that its main antagonists—gargoyles—are not evil, but misunderstood.[43] Designed by Richard Garriott, it represented a significant evolution from his 1980 title *Akalabeth*, whose goal was to "help rid Akalabeth of the foul beasts which infest it." Role-playing video games in general have long given players the option to parley with enemies, including monsters, but they do so very selectively.[44] In *The Witcher 3: Wild Hunt*, for example, only some monsters can be engaged in conversation, while others—often of the same species—need to be avoided or killed.[45] Another notable example of closing the gap between humans and monsters comes from WB Games's *Middle-Earth* series of Tolkien adaptations (*Shadow of Mordor* and *Shadow of War*).[46] Although Tolkien was preoccupied with the morality of the monster slayer, his own work presented the whole monstrous "race" of Orcs as irredeemable servants of evil and cannon fodder for the heroic protagonists—a depiction that has been criticized as a one-dimensional, simplistic example of racial stereotyping.[47] The adaptations humanize Orcs by allowing them to evolve alongside the protagonist, a human ranger named Talion. Orc captains in these games have their strengths, weaknesses, behavioral quirks, and relationships within their ranks that may develop as the game progresses (see figure 4.5). Instead of atomized and transient enemies, these opponents are networked and persistent. If Talion hurts

FIGURE 4.5
Ur-Benu Grog-Maker, an Orc generated by *Shadow of War*'s (2017) Nemesis system.

one with fire, they might, for example, start hating fire and become enraged whenever they are hit by it. If, on the other hand, the captain or his troops manage to kill Talion, they become stronger and rise in the ranks of the Orc army; they will also mock the protagonist during future encounters.

Called the Nemesis system, this set of mechanics gives Orcs a semblance of personal and social life. The system's success can be partly explained by the fact that Orcs are a monstrous race—humanoid but not quite human. The series portrays them as crude, comically over-the-top antagonists who ruthlessly compete for higher ranks and have few interests outside brawling and drinking grog. The game presents merely a caricature of a society but still grants the Orcs more complex lives than are usually granted even to human enemies. While computationally simple, the Nemesis system has been lauded as original and refreshing, with one journalist calling it "the [console] generation's best new mechanic."[48] Despite its positive reception—and despite video game journalists' encouragement of other developers to "steal" or "copy" it—the system has not been widely adopted.[49] Since WB Games patented it in 2021, this is even less likely to happen in the future.[50]

OUT OF SIGHT, OUT OF REACH

The invisible monsters of the Anthropocene cannot be confronted on human terms. As noted by Marianne Gunderson, one can find their predecessors in the genre of weird fiction, "populated by nebulous figures of nonhuman creatures whose alienness is described as irreducible, whose difference is total."[51] This takes us back to the notion of sublime monstrosity. In the previous chapters, I showed how the information about monsters is contained within algorithms and databases and shaped by the development tools at hand. However, the player does not have full access to this information. In his essay on *ludic sublime*, Daniel Vella argues that at the beginning of play, each game is potentially a mystery, even if it may be deciphered along the way. Using the example of *Dark Souls*, he shows how games may choose to preserve this mystery by withholding or obfuscating information.[52] In the words of game scholar Justyna Janik, a game "is not only a digital partner we play with" but may also be "a keeper of secrets."[53] To bolster the sublime qualities of a monster, a game can therefore hide it from the player's view.

A well-known example is the 2010 first-person survival horror title *Amnesia: The Dark Descent* by the Swedish studio Frictional Games.[54] Inspired by the works of H. P. Lovecraft and E. A. Poe, the game follows the story of a male protagonist, Daniel, who explores a Gothic castle to recollect his memories and confront his past. While navigating the creepy hallways and sewers, the player gets sonic cues that monsters—such as Gatherers and Servant Brutes—are nearby, but there is no way of defeating them as the game features no combat. In fact, within the game's *sanity* mechanics, gazing at monsters drains the sanity stat, affecting the representation of game space. The sanity stat already appeared in the 1981 Lovecraftian tabletop RPG *Call of Cthulhu*, but its rendering in *The Dark Descent* is more akin to the 2002 video game *Eternal Darkness: Sanity's Requiem*.[55] When Daniel's sanity is low, his vision becomes blurry and warped, and he may hallucinate horrific sounds and images—including monsters that are not really there. Instead of a quasi-objective photorealistic rendering

of the game's 3D space, *The Dark Descent* offers a more subjective, distorted image, simulating the effects of fear rather
than showing the fearsome things themselves. In my own
playthrough of the game, I avoided looking at monsters so
successfully that I only ever glimpsed them from a distance.
Only later, when browsing the game's wiki, did I first see the
grotesque and disturbing image of the Gatherer's misshapen
jaw—a trademark visual feature of this monster, devised by
the concept artist Jonas Steinick Berlin (see figure 4.6).

Although *The Dark Descent* discourages the player from
looking at monsters, a lot of care went into their visual design
at both the concept art and 3D modelling stage. The Gatherer
exists as a detailed 3D object in the simulated space, but its
Euclidean form tends to be covered by darkness or obscured
by visual filters. Another of the game's monsters—an under-
water creature called Kaernk—is a worthy successor to *Zork*'s
Grue. During regular gameplay, it is effectively invisible, as

FIGURE 4.6
A Gatherer in *Amnesia: The Dark Descent* (2010).

it is constantly submerged in water. Delving into the game's data files, fans have discovered that its in-game 3D model is a simple sphere, although it is not visible anywhere in the game.[56] To the player, the creature's audiovisual representation is purely indexical, as its location can be deduced from the splashes it produces on the water surface. The monsters of *The Dark Descent*, then, defy becoming objects of either sight or action. As the film scholar Adam Charles Hart points out, the game departs "from the otherwise creature-saturated world of video games by restricting the visualization of (and interaction with) monsters."[57] Its approach to monsters goes against the combat-oriented gameplay of most action games but has been used in other survival horror games, including Frictional Games's subsequent releases.

A more recent example of a visible yet inscrutable monster is the Astral Spike from 2019's third-person shooter *Control*, inspired by the genre of "new weird" as well as paranormal-themed stories such as *The X-Files*.[58] Most of the game's enemies are just human agents possessed by an entity called Hiss, but the Astral Spike is quite different. According to the game's lead visual effects artist Elmeri Raitanen, it was "deliberately designed to prevent you from making much sense of it." An in-game document describes the Spikes as "metastructural entities found in the Astral Plane" that "seem to exist beyond our dimension's physical laws." Visually, they could be described as glitchy hairballs of darkness pulsating in a frenetic staccato rhythm (see figure 4.7). Like Kaernk's, Astral Spike's representation is largely indexical. Raitanen notes that the impact of this monster is not "necessarily about how the enemy itself looks" but how it affects the environment— shattering surrounding objects and hurling splinters into the

FIGURE 4.7
The protagonist of *Control* (2019), Jesse Faden, aiming at an Astral Spike.

air like a tornado. Its distinctive look is achieved by combining a procedurally generated simulation made in the visual effects software Houdini with "distorting shard particles, dust and other mesh particles." Contrary to the dominant trend of monstrous realism discussed in the previous chapter, the Astral Spike is no mass, all effect—to the extent that it resembles a bug in the renderer. Its visual design echoes Luckhurst's observation that the monsters of the Anthropocene are defined in terms of an ever-expanding surface without a core that could be analyzed.

Unlike other enemies in the game, an Astral Spike cannot be destroyed. The *Control* art book aptly describes it as a "hazardous 'entity' rather than an enemy," designed to create "an absolute sense of creeping dread."[59] In a mid-game mission, the player must contain a Spike in an enclosed space in order to progress. Several more of them can be found later in the game but cannot be captured and do not even pose a significant threat—they are just *there*, with no other discernible purpose but to be weird. This resonates with *Control*'s narrative, revolving around a government agency that strives to understand and contain paranormal threats but always falls short.[60]

THE SWARM HAS NO FRONT

Posthuman teratology beckons us to look beyond the boundaries of the individual hero or monster and consider instead an unbounded, supra-individual monstrosity that expands in space and time. As Alexander Galloway and Eugene Thacker have noted, "the moments when the network logic takes over—in the mob or the swarm, in contagion or infection—are the moments that are the most disorienting, the most threatening to the integrity of the human ego."[61] Digital technology's capability of generating this kind of monstrosity goes hand in hand with its potential for evoking the experience of computational sublime.[62]

Infection as an invisible monster has a strong thematic presence in postapocalyptic video games. Titles like *The Last of Us* are set in a world devastated by a pandemic. But as Weise has observed, "infection . . . seems to be one of the least portrayed zombie rules, both as a fail state and as a genuine component of a game's rule system."[63] In most mainstream zombie games, a pandemic is merely a back story; infection, if present, is treated as a scripted narrative event rather than a simulated process.[64] However, the recent coronavirus pandemic has taught us that the monstrosity of a virus stems not only from the harm it causes to individuals but also from the elusive dynamic of its rapid spread among the population, which is difficult to grasp without an active knowledge of mathematical functions. Paradoxically, one of the most realistic in-game representations of a pandemic was unintentional; during the 2005 Corrupted Blood incident in the MMORPG *World of Warcraft*, a disease—originally intended to infect a small number of players within an enclosed area—spread across the virtual world due to an unintentional programming oversight. The disease wreaked havoc within the world of the game, forcing players to flee towns and cities in search of safety in uninhabited areas.[65]

The Corrupted Blood incident highlights the capacity of computer technology to generate unforeseen events out of relatively simple rules. This capacity can be described in terms of *emergence*, a concept that describes how "novel properties and capacities emerge from a causal interaction."[66] In game design and game studies, the term is used to label events that result from fixed game mechanics but are neither predetermined nor scripted; emergence can therefore produce unique situations in each playthrough.[67] Conway's *Game of Life*, discussed in chapter 1, is a prime example of such emergence. Emergence also occurs in monster mechanics; the 2006 game *Dead Rising* was among the first to feature vast numbers of zombies, advertising a "next generation 'swarm' technology" that "surrounds you with hundreds of on-screen zombies to hack, drive and run through."[68] While the undead do become targets of joyful destruction, the aggregate behavior of the zombie horde can shift the dynamic of the battle quite abruptly.[69] To quote Weise:

> Zombies [of *Dead Rising*] are so slow, so easy to kill, that beating up on them is a deeply satisfying power trip. Downing one, two, three, even four zombies is much

fun. It's so fun that the player may fail to notice that, in the time it has taken them to kill four zombies, seven more have appeared to their left, twelve have appeared on their right, and a good thirty or forty may have appeared behind them. The player may turn around, triumphant, only to be staring directly into a vast ocean of the undead.[70]

As the label used for *Dead Rising*'s zombie behavior technology suggests, these emergent phenomena can be understood as *swarms*. According to Galloway and Thacker, swarms "throw up a challenge to traditional notions of enmity" because a swarm "has no 'front,' no battle line, no central point of vulnerability"—it is a "faceless foe."[71] In real-life conflict situations, a good example of a swarm is a multipronged cyberattack that lacks a clear leader or agenda. In video games, we are more likely to encounter literal swarms of rodents or insects, traditionally linked to doom and pestilence. Such swarms make for effective monstrosities, but they are not well suited to the player vs. environment model that expects a hero (or a small group) to fight against one or more individual opponents. Games therefore commonly include so-called aggregate monsters that stand in for whole swarms but are handled as singular entities, such as the Seeker Swarms in *Mass Effect 3* or the Flocks in *Gears 5*.[72]

Among the outliers committed to simulating actual swarm behavior is *A Plague Tale: Innocence*, a 2019 action-adventure game that follows the journey of a group of children through plague-infested medieval France. The developers from the French company Asobo Studio decided to set the game during the times of the Black Death but faced the conundrum of "how to represent bubonic plague and make it, well, fun." In other words, they were looking for a suitable metaphor for a contagion. They soon settled on rats, but neither individual specimens nor aggregates would do the trick. As the game director Kevin Choteau has put it: "If we wanted to have this unstoppable force that spreads around the country, destroying everything, it meant we need tonnes of rats, this huge sea of rats . . . Yeah, suddenly the numbers were crazy high."[73] The finished game simulates up to five thousand rats at once, hinting at the computational sublime afforded by contemporary gaming technology (see figure 4.8). The rats' behavior is simulated simply but efficiently, giving a lifelike impression of emergent swarming. Each rat can switch between a finite number of states: they are afraid of light, so they always run away from lamps and torches, and they have insatiable appetite, so they run toward whatever they consider food, including the player characters or their human antagonists.

FIGURE 4.8
The final battle of *A Plague Tale: Innocence* (2019) is fought mostly by proxies—two armies of rats.

Although each rat is stored in the computer memory as a distinct entity, the player learns to treat them as a dynamic, flowing mass that can be controlled with strategically placed light sources or food items and can be directed to kill other enemies or assist in solving puzzles.

The rats of *A Plague Tale: Innocence* create the illusion of coordinated movement because they all follow the same stimuli. But we can also imagine beings that possess a collective consciousness or collective intelligence. These two concepts, which found their way from the natural and social sciences to science fiction and fantasy, offer an antithesis to modernist individualism and can be seen as both utopian and monstrous (the latter in the case of *Star Trek*'s Borg).[74] In role-playing and video games, the Cranium Rat provides a handy example. The creature was first designed for *Planescape*, a 1994 campaign setting for *D&D* that introduced a fantasy world much weirder than the Tolkienesque fantasy of the original *D&D* settings. Cranium Rats are depicted as rats whose brains are partially exposed, granting them telepathic powers:

> They're many creatures and one creature all at once, as they possess a type of group mind. A cranium rat is automatically in telepathic contact with every other such creature within 10 feet, which allows them to share not just thoughts, but also brain capacity—every five rats in contact generate 1 point of Intelligence.[75]

As a result, one hundred Cranium Rats would possess twenty Intelligence points, making them as sharp as the best humanoid magicians. Cranium Rat swarms can telepathically speak to the player characters as one creature, "referring to itself using the collective pronouns 'we' and 'us.'"[76] In the 1999 computer game adaptation *Planescape: Torment*, large groups of Cranium Rats are capable of casting powerful attack spells and rank among the game's fiercest (and most surprising) enemies.[77] At the same time, the protagonist may negotiate and ally himself with a Cranium Rat collective, which refers to itself as "Many-As-One." This video game implementation of the Cranium Rat is rather rudimentary and might not instill the feeling of computational sublime in a way that *A Plague Tale: Innocence* does. Nevertheless, it remains one of the most original creatures in gaming. It cleverly questions the intellectual primacy of the human subject and presents a fluid monstrosity whose attributes can shift dynamically during an encounter.

BREAKING OUT OF THE MACHINE

When fighting on-screen monsters, we tend to look past the interface, past the hardware and its operating system, and past the game's software. Most of the time, we treat them as disinterested machinery that delivers a pleasurable experience and acts as an impartial referee. But if we are to find the sublime in video games, Eugénie Shinkle suggests, we need to look for it "at those points in gameplay where the player becomes aware of the technology that lies beneath the game form, and where the consequences of this encounter present a challenge to the self." Shinkle gives examples of glitches and failure events that reveal the game as "an inexpressive intelligence, a pure, depersonalized power, a technological other."[78]

While unintended glitches can surely be understood as monstrous, designers can also purposefully create the illusion that the gaming hardware and software have been possessed by a monster. Perhaps the most famous example is the battle against Psycho Mantis, who first appeared as a mid-game boss in the 1998 stealth-action game *Metal Gear Solid*.[79] Although a human by birth, Psycho Mantis hides his humanity behind a full-body leather suit and a gas mask. Upon meeting the game's protagonist, Solid Snake, Psycho Mantis boasts supernatural powers and claims to be "the most powerful practitioner of psychokinesis and telepathy in the world." To demonstrate, he "reads" the player's memories by accessing savegame blocks on the PlayStation memory card and commenting on the titles he has found. Then, he asks the player to lay the controller on the floor and claims that he can make it move "by the power of [his] will alone" (in fact the program achieves that by using the controller's rumble feature). When the fight commences, Psycho Mantis avoids Solid Snake's attacks by supposedly reading his mind. The trick is to unplug the controller and re-plug it into the other controller port.

This disorienting—and amusing—sequence is routinely listed among the most memorable moments in gaming.[80] According to Stephanie Boluk and Patrick Lemieux, it constitutes one of the "defamiliarizing moments in *Metal Gear* [that] foreground the platform and larger media apparatus of video games."[81] In popular discourse, such narrative transgressions are commonly described as "breaking the fourth wall." Steven Conway retorts that rather than *breaking*, we should speak of *expansion*, as the imaginary wall between the player and the game "expands outwards to absorb whatever the game developer deems appropriate to enhance the immersive quality of the game."[82] Psycho Mantis temporarily gains control over the machine, reaches into the real-world gameplay situation, and addresses the player rather than the protagonist. The experience severely disrupts the flow of the game, combining a failure of distancing (as we have lost the safe buffer space of the interface) with a failure of engagement (as we have lost the ability to meaningfully interact with the game world). At this moment, we may realize that the game's hardware and software are not just reliable intermediaries but can also be in league with the monster. Fittingly for a series critical of the military-industrial complex, *Metal Gear* shatters the Cold War–era notion that enmity can be contained within the closed worlds of military simulation and points out that the simulation itself can become monstrous.

Similar design tricks have been used in several other games including *Undertale*. Its infamous antagonist Flowey can access the history of player actions and cruelly mocks the player for their decisions (even if they had tried to take them back by reloading). At the end of the game, Flowey even claims to have destroyed the player's save file and initiates a boss battle unlike any other in the game. While all the other monsters are black and white, Flowey transforms into a grotesque organic abomination rendered in colorful, photorealistic graphics of a kind that appears nowhere else in the game; in fact, Fox purposely commissioned the graphics work from an outside collaborator with the explicit instruction to make Flowey "unsettling."[83] All of this contributes to the impression that Flowey is able to break from containment and transcend both the interface and the fictional world of the game (see figures 4.9 and 4.10).[84]

The abovementioned intrusions are brief and reversible, creating an illusion of daemons that were let loose and temporarily became bugs. They are also ostentatious, leaving no doubt that the fourth wall has been expanded.[85] It is, however, technically possible to unleash a monster that plays

FIGURES 4.9 AND 4.10

The first encounter with *Undertale*'s (2015) Flowey the flower and his boss monster version, called "Photoshop Flowey" by the fan community.

similar mind tricks for dozens of hours. This was the case with the 2014 first-person horror title *Alien: Isolation*, developed by the British studio Creative Assembly.[86] Aiming to "make the Alien scary again," the team took inspiration from the original 1979 Ridley Scott movie, even casting Amanda Ripley, the daughter of the original tetralogy's protagonist Ellen Ripley, as the main character.[87] Following up on the model pioneered by *3D Monster Maze*, the developers scrapped the multitudes of aliens found in some previous games in the franchise and replaced them with a single, recurring, and undefeatable Alien. *Isolation*'s monster was advertised as "an enemy that you need to avoid at all costs. An Alien that is stalking you; that's intelligent, unpredictable, extremely dangerous."[88]

The in-game Alien is controlled by an AI module that uses *behavior trees* to execute specific behaviors under certain sets of conditions, such as running to inspect a location when detecting noise. However, additional behaviors unlock throughout the game—if a player keeps hiding in the lockers, for example, the monster will start opening them. This way, the game creates the illusion that the Alien is learning without using genuine machine learning algorithms. Besides the Alien module, there is another one called the Director, designed to maintain gameplay tension without pre-scripted jump scares. It aims for an experience described as "psychopathic serendipity"—meaning that the monster appears whenever the player might feel like they have finally evaded it. The Director module periodically provides the Alien module with information about the whereabouts of the player, prompting another encounter. As the video game AI specialist Tommy Thompson put it: "The [Alien] in *Alien: Isolation* has two brains: one that always knows where you are and gives hints to the second that controls the body."[89]

My previously published research into the reception of the game has shown that some players considered the interaction between the Director and the Alien unfair and complained that the Alien "cheated." In other words, these players believe that despite being simulated by the game's software, the monster should not have unbridled access to the data about the state of the simulated world and should only follow its simulated sensory perception.[90] In their analysis of the game, Brendan Keogh and Darshana Jayemanne view *Isolation*'s Alien as a bug rather than a daemon, writing that it "feels less like a ludic challenge to learn, overcome and enjoy, and more like an intentional, unpredictable and malicious glitch in the system to be avoided at all cost."[91] Some players, however, found the encounters repetitive and annoying; relatively few people finished the game to the end.[92] While *3D Monster Maze* could be played as a series of short matches, it is more difficult to fit such an invincible opponent into a title that—following the contemporary conventions of mainstream single-player games—takes dozens of hours to beat. In the end, *Isolation*'s unique approach to monster behavior did not translate into a commercial success, making it unlikely that such an experiment will be repeated any time soon in the mainstream video game industry.

The examples in this chapter have shown that the video game medium offers ample potential for articulating more nuanced and contemporary forms of monstrosity. While games like *Shadow of the Colossus* reframe monsters through narrative and world-building, titles such as *A Plague Tale:*

Innocence employ technological innovations that aim for the computational sublime. Another promising direction in monster technology—randomized procedural generation—has already been broached by games such as *No Man's Sky*.[93] But the way toward fresh monsters may also involve the subtraction rather than the addition of features. *Zork*'s Grue remains scary because the game has no graphics at all; *Control*'s Astral Spike is impressive in part because it lacks combat mechanics.

Although this book focuses primarily on monstrous adversaries, it is worth noting that games may also cast monsters as protagonists or companions, letting players explore otherness from the subject perspective. *D&D*, admittedly a "human-centric" game at its inception, ended up considerably expanding the selection of playable "races." The recent fan expansion *Monstrous Races* even offers instructions on how to play and role-play all monsters from the fifth-edition *D&D Monster Manual*, including the Gelatinous Cube, and even animated objects, including the Flying Sword or the (rather ominous) Rug of Smothering. This makes the volume a captivating vernacular articulation of posthuman teratology. Video games may likewise simulate the monster's perspective. As noted by Jonne Arjoranta in his analysis of the 2010 game *Aliens vs. Predator*, they tend to do so by altering the game's sounds or visuals, by adding or subtracting the information available to the player, and by granting the protagonist special powers.[94] The Alien in this game can, for example, "smell" humans, a trait that the game represents by displaying outlines around human characters, even if they are behind a wall. There are obvious limitations to portraying an alien experience. As famously argued by the philosopher Thomas Nagel on the example of a bat, it is impossible for humans to experience or imagine what it is like to be a different species because our sensory perception is structured in a radically different way.[95] Moreover, Arjoranta suggests that "a game focused on conveying the embodied experience of something completely alien would not be particularly playable," once again pointing to the game design conventions that shape our ideas of what is an enjoyable game.[96] Recently, the ambitious independent game *Carrion* has let one play as an insatiable tentacle monster. As a 2D action-puzzle hybrid, it does not truly attempt to convey the embodied experience of being a tentacle monster, but it does explore novel types of agency and navigation.[97]

Despite the opportunities, there is still a lot of untapped potential in representing and designing video game monsters. Innovative monstrosity does not necessarily require advanced technology, but it does call for a deeper reflection of the technological foundations and design conventions of the medium. The slow (or nonexistent) uptake of mechanical innovation exemplified by the *Middle-Earth* games' Nemesis system and *Isolation*'s AI suggests that attempts at original monster mechanics clash with the genre conventions and production processes of the video game industry. Game development—both corporate and independent—is a notoriously risky business, and sticking to time-tested formulas reduces the risk.[98] The ongoing economic consolidation of the game industry is unlikely to change that, as it seems to be driven by the desire to capitalize on existing intellectual property rather than to provide an environment for creative experimentation. When inventing new monsters, then, one must also fight the behemoths of business and the stone giants of calcified clichés.

CONCLUSION

In March 2021, as a major wave of COVID-19 infections subsided in the United States, the *Washington Post* published a piece with the headline: "They laughed, they cried, they killed monsters: How friendships thrived in video games during the pandemic." Based on interviews with players and academics, the article reported that video games provide a reason for people to get together online and socialize. Interestingly, though, many of the games featured in the article, such as *FIFA 21*, *Animal Crossing*, or *Among Us*, do not feature any monsters at all. As I have suggested throughout this book, the expression "killing monsters" remains a convenient signifier for gaming in general. It has come to stand in for an ordinary, even wholesome and therapeutic activity—a comfort food of gaming. This book has offered clues as to why and how this has happened. I set out to answer two basic questions: How did monsters become such an emblematic part of the video game medium? And how has the medium, in turn, transformed the concept of monstrosity? The individual chapters have revealed the pieces of the puzzle, and all that remains is to assemble them.

First, I explored theories of monstrosity, finding that the sublime thesis—common in the classic Western thinking about the subject—falls short of explaining the appeal and the functions of video game monsters. To understand those, we must also consider the parallel tendencies to decipher and contain the unknown. This impulse became especially strong in the post–World War II era, as entertainment industries set out to commodify monstrosity on a massive scale, creating a monster culture that was in parts playful and consumerist. Around the same time, the military-scientific complex introduced technologies designed to simulate and predict conflict scenarios, setting the scene for an invasion of fictional hostile monsters.

The notion of killing monsters as a common gameplay activity is a relatively recent innovation, resulting from a confluence of technological, ideological, and cultural developments in the postwar decades. The rise of monsters was inextricably tied to the emergence of the player vs. environment mode of gameplay in the 1970s, exemplified by *D&D* and *Space Invaders*. Digital technology played a central role in the proliferation of the player vs. environment formula, but it was not the only factor. As the example of *D&D*—which did not require a computer—shows, the conceptual framework involving simulation, calculation, and databases was more important than the technology itself. Soon thereafter, monsters became a ubiquitous type of antagonist in computerized entertainment. They provided a catchy, convenient, and ever-expandable category of video game content while also helping designers avoid the uncomfortable moral issue of killing simulated humans.

The second question I asked was how video games have transformed the notion of the monster. At its core, the answer is twofold: monsters have been simulated and objectified.

Unlike the creatures of literature or film, video games monsters are almost invariably simulated models, constructed from well-defined data and procedures. H. P. Lovecraft could convey a monstrous image with a series of vague adjectives; the special effects personnel for Ridley Scott's *Alien* (1979) only had to create those parts of the monster that were visible in individual camera takes.[1] The monsters of contemporary 3D video games are more akin to the miniature skeletons created by Ray Harryhausen for *Jason and the Argonauts*: they need to be fabricated as 3D sculptures with a full range of motion. Moreover, they must be assigned sets of rules that allow them to interact with the player and the simulated world.

The other transformation of monstrosity—its objectification—already started with the practices of predigital monster culture, such as miniature collecting. In video games, the objectification resulted in monsters becoming targets of player agency—enemies and playthings that need to be figured out and destroyed. In accordance with the design ideology of flow, player vs. environment video games require a steady stream of opponents that can be dispatched for player satisfaction. Video games have therefore caused a quantitative explosion of monsters—both in terms of types and individual specimens. Although boss monsters are unique and may interrupt flow of gameplay, even they are designed to be beaten.

Any evaluation of these changes depends on the normative stance one takes toward monstrosity. Along with many authors cited in this book, including Jeffrey Jerome Cohen or Patricia MacCormack, I believe that the cultural value of monstrosity derives from the fact that it holds up a mirror to humanity and questions our knowledge of the world around us.[2] From that perspective, much of video game monster design seems like a wasted opportunity. The conventions of the player vs. environment model curb monstrosity's potential for complexity and smooth its transgressive edge in the service of player empowerment. Player vs. environment gameplay tends to promote the simplistic and outdated perception of otherness as something that can be predicted, destroyed, and turned into in-game capital. To use a tech industry buzzword that has been widely criticized in academic game studies, monstrosity has been *gamified*—translated into a system of points, achievements, and rewards.[3]

On the other hand, the creature craze triggered by *D&D* and video games has also opened doors to many imaginative, playful, and disturbing monster designs. Chapter 3 showcased the creative work of monster designers and the imprints they leave on their creations. In chapter 4, I identified games that show more complex and thought-provoking kinds of monstrosity—by casting doubt on the heroism of the hero and on the monstrosity of the monsters, or by presenting monsters that are elusive, indifferent, emergent, or glitchy. While such examples are quite rare, that might make them even more effective.

ALL THE WORLD'S MONSTERS?

Despite its promises, video game monster design has been criticized for its lack of inventiveness, as well as for stereotypical representations of gendered, racialized, or ethnic otherness.[4] In part, these deficiencies reflect the game industry's tendency to avoid risk by building on existing franchises and genre templates; they can also be explained by the industry's lack of diversity. While the selection of examples in this book is hardly representative of the whole sector, the designers mentioned here are overwhelmingly male, with women relegated to professions traditionally coded as more feminine, such as visual artists or animators.[5]

If we look at regional diversity, the picture is a bit more ambiguous. On the one hand, video game monster design is an international undertaking. Out of the two foundational titles of player vs. environment gameplay, one was produced in the United States (*D&D*) and the other in Japan (*Space Invaders*). Besides these two countries, other notable titles from this book were made by developers from the United Kingdom (*3D Monster Maze, Alien: Isolation*), France (*A Plague Tale: Innocence*), Sweden (*Amnesia: The Dark Descent*), and Finland (*Control*). Many monster designs, both audiovisual and mechanical, arose from transnational exchange: early *D&D* looked for inspiration in bootleg miniatures inspired by the *Ultraman* TV series, while Taito's *Space Invaders* was inspired by Atari's *Breakout*.[6]

On the other hand, the cultural influences skew heavily toward Anglo-Saxon and Japanese popular culture and Greco-Roman and Germanic mythology. Much of the contemporary monstrous canon draws on J. R. R. Tolkien's and H. P. Lovecraft's fiction, George Romero's and Ray Harryhausen's films, and the Japanese kaiju tradition. Teams from other regions nevertheless try to differentiate their work by using monsters from local cultures: the *Witcher* series as well as the more recent indie title *Black Book* both contain creatures from Slavic mythology, such as the Noonwraith (a female demon who abducts children at noon) or the Leshy (a forest guardian spirit who is himself part tree).[7] The Philippine horror game *Nightfall: Escape*, too, adapts local folk monsters, such as the Manananggal (a vampire-like being with a taste for human viscera and fetuses) or the Batibat (a grotesquely obese tree spirit).[8]

Despite the inclusion of local themes, today's game production is such a globalized endeavor that it is difficult to make general claims about regional trends in portraying video game monsters. Take the example of Japan. Its Shinto religion, whose influence has a strong imprint in contemporary popular culture, is hospitable to spirits and supernatural beings. In contrast to the Greco-Roman and medieval European association of monsters with outside threats, Japanese folk monsters—called *yōkai*—co-inhabit the world with humans, albeit in a delicate tension.[9] One might therefore expect Japanese video games to treat monsters with more nuance and empathy. While examples like *Bloodborne*, *Shadow of the Colossus*, or *Metal Gear Solid* fulfill that expectation, there is also the *Monster Hunter* series—unapologetically colonialist and anthropocentric.[10]

BLANK PAGES IN THE BESTIARY

While writing this book, I have often pondered how different languages offer different ways of speaking about monsters. As a Czech scholar writing in English, I miss the range of synonyms for monsters offered by the Czech language. Besides the Latin loanword *monstrum* (monster), these include the words *potvora*, *příšera*, *obluda*, *zrůda*, *stvůra*, *nestvůra*, and *netvor*, each varying slightly as to the kind and degree of monstrosity.[11] The English synonyms such as *critter*, *beast*, *fiend*, *aberration*, or *abomination*, on the other hand, are all very specific and barely overlap. While I felt constrained by English vocabulary, perhaps my knowledge of Czech attuned me to a few more shades of monstrosity. More importantly, this reflection has helped me realize how much my perspective on the topic is shaped by my cultural and academic background and by my gaming history.

The study of monsters presented in this book is limited not only by the languages I can read but also by the literature and the material I worked with. Most of the theory and concepts I have used—including the notions of the sublime, the grotesque, or realism—are of Western origin and may not capture the nuances of monstrosity in other cultures. As for material, I have tried to cover a wide range of historical and contemporary examples, but I have nevertheless gravitated to the titles that I know from my own player practice. As a result, there are segments of gaming that this book has not covered. One of them is the MMORPG genre, with its epic "raid bosses" that can only be beaten by large and well-coordinated groups of players. Another is the genre of strategy games, which offers great potential for monster design thanks to its focus on multitudes rather than individual entities.

Due to space constraints, I have not covered contemporary nondigital games, many of which can offer unique portrayals and experiences of monstrosity: In titles such as *Kingdom Death: Monster*, players control characters that fight monsters but also take turns controlling the monsters, allowing them to observe and act from both perspectives; the card game *Hecatomb*—a weirder relative of *Magic: The Gathering*—embraces posthuman monstrosity by letting players build fluid and unstable abominations out of individual monsters.[12] Along with the abovementioned genres, proper academic treatment should be given to monstrous protagonists, whom I relegated to a short note in the previous chapter, as well as to monstrous companions.

Video game monsters, in general, deserve much more academic scrutiny, both theoretical and empirical. Luckily, the interest in studying them is on the rise. In April 2021, the Tampere University Game Research Lab organized their annual spring seminar around the theme of monstrosity.[13] As a participant and commentator, I was struck by the variety of approaches to monsters. There were critiques of monstrous representations in games—particularly in terms of gender or race—and examinations of folkloric inspirations as well as colonialism in monster design; one study dove deep into sound design for monsters. The methods included close readings, online forum studies, quantitative corpus analysis, and ethnographies. Only six months later, in October 2021, the journal *Analog Game Studies* published a special issue dedicated to the *Fiend Folio*, a 1981 *D&D* rulebook that served as an expansion of the 1979 *Monster Manual*.[14] All of this suggests that monsters have found a firm place in game scholarship's research agenda.

A FUTURE FOR MONSTERS

While charting the possible futures of monster research, we should not forget about the future of monsters themselves. One of my aims in this book has been to historicize and contextualize the role of monsters in video games and to explain that their prominence in the medium is not a given. What does that mean for their future? Will there even be new monsters to study? Or will "killing monsters" become a fossilized metonym that no longer corresponds to contemporary gaming practice?

Over the last decade, there have been signs that players might enjoy beating other players more than beating simulated enemies. The impact of highly profitable competitive multi-player games like *League of Legends*, *Overwatch*, and *Fortnite* has led some journalists and industry experts to predict the end of single-player games.[15] If that were to happen, would that also spell the end of video game monsters? Would there still be place for them if people preferred to play against each other? In fact, the situation is much more complicated. Given how quickly trends shift in the game industry, announcing the end of anything is almost always premature, and some commentators have already noticed a rebound of single-player games.[16] More importantly: as I have pointed out in chapter 2, the categories of single and multiplayer games do not align with the categories of the player vs. environment and player vs. player modes of play. Many of the recent multi-player hits, such as *Fortnite* and *League of Legends*, involve fighting monstrous opponents, although their main challenge is to defeat other players.[17]

Rather than player vs. player games replacing player vs. environment ones, the two are likely to converge. In her discussion of player vs. environment games, Alenda Y. Chang finds this scenario plausible, "not just because networked online play is more readily available now or because games themselves have become more complex, but because mastery over nature and mastery over other people are increasingly one and the same thing."[18] Although the future is likely to bring new types of social play, simulated environments and simulated entities are unlikely to disappear. Barring a sudden drop in popularity of fantasy, science fiction, and horror, a good portion of these simulated entities will always be represented as monstrous.

If monsters do remain an integral part of gaming, one might wonder what they will be like. Since that is ultimately up to the designers, developers, and game industry executives to decide, let us ask another question instead: What kinds of monsters do we wish for? The previous chapter has given us some important pointers. Such monsters could affect us in new, unexpected ways and complicate the simple opposition of "us against them." As Alenda Y. Chang has noted, "what we truly need are games where the player is *in*, *of*, or *with* the environment" rather than just "versus" the environment.[19] To return to the original meaning of the word, a monstrum is "that which warns" or "that which reveals." Perhaps we might wish for monsters that warn us against anthropocentric hubris and that make us reflect on who we are as players—and humans.

NOTES

INTRODUCTION

1. Ken St. Andre, *Tunnels & Trolls* (1975; 1st ed. repr., Phoenix, AZ: Flying Buffalo, 2013), 8.

2. Joy Lisi Rankin, *A People's History of Computing in the United States* (Cambridge, MA: Harvard University Press, 2018).

3. *Dnd*, v. 5.4, (Gary Whisenhunt, Ray Wood, Dirk Pellett, and Flint Pellett, 1977), PLATO.

4. *Space Invaders* (Taito, 1978), arcade; *God of War* (Sony Interactive Entertainment, 2018), PS4.

5. Margrit Shildrick, *Embodying the Monster: Encounters with the Vulnerable Self*, Theory, Culture & Society (London: SAGE Publications, 2002).

6. Donna Haraway, "The Promises of Monsters: A Regenerative Politics for Inappropriate/d Others," in *Cultural Studies*, ed. Lawrence Grossberg, Cary Nelson, and Paula A. Treichler (New York: Routledge, 1992), 295–336.

7. Noël Carroll, *The Philosophy of Horror: Or, Paradoxes of the Heart* (New York: Routledge, 1990), 27. Carroll's definition purposefully includes extinct species such as dinosaurs.

8. Diane Carr, "Textual Analysis, Digital Games, Zombies," in *Proceedings of the 2009 DiGRA International Conference: Breaking New Ground:*

Innovation in Games, Play, Practice and Theory (Digital Games Research Association, 2009), http://www.digra.org/wp-content/uploads/digital -library/09287.241711.pdf; Matthew J. Weise, "How the Zombie Changed Videogames," in *Zombies Are Us: Essays on the Humanity of the Walking Dead*, ed. Christopher M. Moreman and Cory Rushton (Jefferson, NC: McFarland, 2011), 151–168; Hans-Joachim Backe and Espen J. Aarseth, "Ludic Zombies: An Examination of Zombieism in Games," in *Proceedings of the 2013 DiGRA International Conference: DeFragging Game Studies* (Digital Games Research Association, 2013), http://www .digra.org/wp-content/uploads/digital-library/paper_405.pdf; Stephen J. Webley and Peter Zackariasson, eds., *The Playful Undead and Video Games: Critical Analyses of Zombies and Gameplay*, Routledge Advances in Game Studies (New York: Routledge, 2020).

9. Bernard Perron, *The World of Scary Video Games: A Study in Videoludic Horror* (New York: Bloomsbury Academic, 2018); Tanya Krzywinska, "The Gamification of Gothic Coordinates in Videogames," *Revenant* 1, no. 1 (2015): 58–78; Tanya Krzywinska, "Gaming Horror's Horror: Representation, Regulation, and Affect in Survival Horror Videogames," *Journal of Visual Culture* 14, no. 3 (December 2015): 293–297, https:// doi.org/10.1177/1470412915607924; Tanya Krzywinska, "Gothic American Gaming," in *The Cambridge Companion to American Gothic*, ed. Jeffrey Andrew Weinstock (Cambridge: Cambridge University Press, 2017), 229–242.

10. Carly A. Kocurek, "Who Hearkens to the Monster's Scream? Death, Violence and the Veil of the Monstrous in Video Games," *Visual Studies* 30, no. 1 (January 2015): 79–89, https://doi.org/10.1080/1472586X .2015.996402.

11. Sarah Stang, "Shrieking, Biting, and Licking: The Monstrous-Feminine and Abject Female Monsters in Video Games," *Press Start* 4, no. 2 (January 2018): 18–34; Sarah Stang, "Big Daddies and Their Little Sisters: Postfeminist Fatherhood in the Bioshock Series," in *Beyond the Sea: Navigating BioShock*, ed. Felan Parker and Jessica Aldred (Montreal: McGill-Queen's University Press, 2018), 27–49; Sarah Stang, "The Broodmother as Monstrous-Feminine—Abject Maternity in Video Games," *Nordlit*, no. 42 (November 2019): 233–256, https://doi.org/10.7557/13.5014; Sarah Stang and Aaron Trammell, "The Ludic Bestiary: Misogynistic Tropes

of Female Monstrosity in *Dungeons & Dragons*," *Games and Culture* 15, no. 6 (2020): 730–747, https://doi.org/10.1177/1555412019850059; Bonnie Ruberg, "Straight-Washing 'Undertale': Video Games and the Limits of LGBTQ Representation," *Transformative Works and Cultures* 28 (September 2018), https://doi.org/10.3983/twc.2018.1516.

12. Olli Sotamaa and Jan Švelch, eds., *Game Production Studies* (Amsterdam: Amsterdam University Press, 2021), https://doi.org/10.5117/9789463725439.

13. A portion of this research has been published in Jaroslav Švelch, "Should the Monster Play Fair?: Reception of Artificial Intelligence in Alien: Isolation," *Game Studies* 20, no. 2 (June 2020), http://gamestudies.org/2002/articles/jaroslav_svelch.

CHAPTER 1

1. Jacques Derrida, "Some Statements and Truisms about Neologisms, Newisms, Postisms, Parasitisms, and Other Small Seismisms," in *The States of "Theory,"* ed. David Carroll, trans. Anne Tomiche (New York: Columbia University Press, 1990), 80.

2. FromSoftware, *Bloodborne* (Sony Computer Entertainment, 2015), PS4. For a review that mentions monster design, see Michael McWhertor, "Bloodborne Review: Scarlett Letter," *Polygon*, March 27, 2015, https://www.polygon.com/2015/3/27/8209199/bloodborne-review-PS4-playstation-4-exclusive.

3. Jeffrey Jerome Cohen, "Monster Culture (Seven Theses)," in *Monster Theory: Reading Culture*, ed. Jeffrey Jerome Cohen (Minneapolis: University of Minnesota Press, 1996), 4.

4. Stephen T. Asma, *On Monsters: An Unnatural History of Our Worst Fears* (Oxford: Oxford University Press, 2012), 192.

5. Immanuel Kant, *Critique of Judgement*, ed. Nicholas Walker, trans. James Creed Meredith, Oxford World's Classics (Oxford: Oxford University Press, 2007), 76.

6. Torill Elvira Mortensen and Kristine Jørgensen, *The Paradox of Transgression in Games* (New York: Routledge, 2020), 172.

7. Jos de Mul, "The (Bio)Technological Sublime," *Diogenes* 59, no. 1–2 (February 2012): 34, https://doi.org/10.1177/0392192112469162.

8. Timothy K. Beal, *Religion and Its Monsters* (New York: Routledge, 2002), 4.

9. Beal, 27.

10. Julia Kristeva, *Powers of Horror: An Essay on Abjection*, European Perspectives (New York: Columbia University Press, 1982), 4.

11. Kristeva, 3.

12. Noël Carroll, *The Philosophy of Horror: Or, Paradoxes of the Heart* (New York: Routledge, 1990), 33.

13. Carroll, 32.

14. Carroll, 45.

15. Stephanie Dalley, ed., *Myths from Mesopotamia: Creation, the Flood, Gilgamesh, and Others*, rev. ed., Oxford World's Classics (Oxford: Oxford University Press, 2000), 236.

16. Beal, *Religion and Its Monsters*.

17. Ruth Waterhouse, "Beowulf as Palimpsest," in *Monster Theory: Reading Culture*, ed. Jeffrey Jerome Cohen (Minneapolis: University of Minnesota Press, 1996), 26–39.

18. Howard Phillips Lovecraft, *Supernatural Horror in Literature* (Mineola, NY: Dover Publications, 1973), 12.

19. Howard Phillips Lovecraft, *Tales of H. P. Lovecraft*, ed. Joyce Carol Oates (New York: HarperPerennial, 2007), 5.

20. See Dan Pinchbeck, "POCG2016 Dan Pinchbeck The Unreliable Philosophics of The Chinese Room," Philosophy of Computer Games Lectures, May 2, 2017, YouTube video, 1:04:14, https://www.youtube.com/watch?v=YqFjBWeNLRY.

21. Asa Simon Mittman, *Maps and Monsters in Medieval England*, Studies in Medieval History and Culture (New York: Routledge, 2006).

22. Willene B. Clark, *A Medieval Book of Beasts: The Second-Family Bestiary: Commentary, Art, Text and Translation* (Woodbridge, UK: Boydell Press, 2006), 194.

23. Richard E. Strassberg, ed., *A Chinese Bestiary: Strange Creatures from the Guideways through Mountains and Seas* (Berkeley: University of California Press, 2002), 9.

24. Zilia Papp, *Anime and Its Roots in Early Japanese Monster Art* (Folkestone, UK: Global Oriental, 2010); Joseph H. Peterson, *The Lesser Key of Solomon: Lemegeton Clavicula Salomonis* (York Beach, ME: Samuel Weiser, 2001).

25. Eugene Thacker, *Tentacles Longer than Night*, Horror of Philosophy 3 (Winchester, UK: Zer0 Books, 2015), 23.

26. *Dante's Inferno* (Electronic Arts, 2010), PS3. Dante likewise inspired the Japanese action game series *Devil May Cry* and gave the name to its protagonist; see *Devil May Cry* (Capcom, 2001), PS2.

27. Margrit Shildrick, "Visual Rhetorics and the Seductions of the Monstrous: Some Precautionary Observations," *Somatechnics* 8, no. 2 (September 2018): 167, https://doi.org/10.3366/soma.2018.0248.

28. Inge Kleivan and Birgitte Sonne, *Eskimos—Greenland and Canada*, Iconography of Religions, Arctic Peoples, Volume: 2 (Leiden, Netherlands: E. J. Brill, 1985), 23.

29. Sheila Romalis, "The East Greenland Tupilaq Image: Old and New Visions," *Études/Inuit/Studies* 7, no. 1 (1983): 152–159.

30. Mortensen and Jørgensen, *Paradox of Transgression*, 3–4.

31. Cohen, "Monster Culture," 4.

32. Roger Luckhurst, *Zombies: A Cultural History* (London: Reaktion Books, 2015).

33. See, for example, Joseph Campbell, *The Hero with a Thousand Faces*, Commemorative ed., Bollingen Series 17 (Princeton, NJ: Princeton University Press, 2004); Ian Jobling, "The Psychological Foundations of the Hero-Ogre Story: A Cross-Cultural Study," *Human Nature*

12, no. 3 (September 2001): 247–272, https://doi.org/10.1007/s12110 -001-1009-7.

34. Debra Higgs Strickland, "Monstrosity and Race in the Late Middle Ages," in *The Ashgate Research Companion to Monsters and the Monstrous*, ed. Asa Simon Mittman and Peter Dendle (Farnham, UK: Ashgate, 2013), 386, https://doi.org/10.4324/9781315241197.ch17.

35. H. L. Malchow, "Frankenstein's Monster and Images of Race in Nineteenth-Century Britain," *Past & Present* 139, no. 1 (May 1993): 90–130, https://doi.org/10.1093/past/139.1.90.

36. James Kneale, "From beyond: H. P. Lovecraft and the Place of Horror," *Cultural Geographies* 13, no. 1 (January 2006): 106–126, https://doi.org/10.1191/1474474005eu353oa.

37. Barbara Creed, *The Monstrous-Feminine: Film, Feminism, Psycho-analysis*, Popular Fiction Series (London: Routledge, 1993).

38. Sarah Stang, "The Broodmother as Monstrous-Feminine—Abject Maternity in Video Games," *Nordlit*, no. 42 (November 2019): 233–256, https://doi.org/10.7557/13.5014.

39. Clark, *Medieval Book of Beasts*.

40. Clive Hart, *Kites: An Historical Survey*, rev. 2nd ed. (Mount Vernon, NY: Paul P. Appel, 1982).

41. Roger Caillois, *Man, Play, and Games* (Urbana: University of Illinois Press, 2001); Johan Huizinga, *Homo Ludens: A Study of the Play-Element in Culture* (London: Routledge & Kegan Paul, 1949).

42. Caillois, *Man, Play, and Games*, 4.

43. Mortensen and Jørgensen, *Paradox of Transgression*, 183.

44. Malcolm Evans and J. K. Greye, *3D Monster Maze* (J. K. Greye Software, 1982), ZX81.

45. Henry Jenkins, *Comics and Stuff* (New York: New York University Press, 2020), 196–197.

46. The song was attributed to Bobby (Boris) Pickett and the Crypt-Kickers and released as a single on the Garpax Records label.

47. Emil Ferris, *My Favorite Thing Is Monsters* (Seattle, WA: Fantagraphics Books, 2017).

48. Bob Rehak, "Materializing Monsters: Aurora Models, Garage Kits and the Object Practices of Horror Fandom," *The Journal of Fandom Studies* 1, no. 1 (November 2012): 30, https://doi.org/10.1386/jfs.1.1.27_1.

49. See Anne Allison, *Millennial Monsters: Japanese Toys and the Global Imagination* (Berkeley: University of California Press, 2006).

50. Hiroki Azuma, *Otaku: Japan's Database Animals*, English ed. (Minneapolis: University of Minnesota Press, 2009).

51. Monster in My Pocket Monstrous 24 Pack, Limited Edition Series I Assortment A. Collection of the Strong Museum of Play, item no. 114.3958.

52. Allison, *Millennial Monsters*, 220.

53. Janet H. Murray, *Hamlet on the Holodeck: The Future of Narrative in Cyberspace* (Cambridge, MA: MIT Press, 1998), 84.

54. Peter Dendle, "Conclusion: Monsters and the Twenty-First Century: The Preternatural in an Age of Scientific Consensus," in *The Ashgate Research Companion to Monsters and the Monstrous*, ed. Asa Simon Mittman and Peter Dendle, Ashgate Research Companions (Farnham, UK: Ashgate, 2013), 437.

55. Allison, *Millennial Monsters*, 217.

56. Ulrich Beck, "World Risk Society and Manufactured Uncertainties," *Iris. European Journal of Philosophy and Public Debate* 1, no. 2 (2009), https://www.torrossa.com/en/resources/an/2489448.

57. James Franklin, *The Science of Conjecture: Evidence and Probability before Pascal*, paperback ed., A Johns Hopkins Paperback (Baltimore: Johns Hopkins University Press, 2015), 274.

58. Jon Peterson, *Playing at the World: A History of Simulating Wars, People and Fantastic Adventures, from Chess to Role-Playing Games* (San Diego: Unreason Press, 2013), 229.

59. Patrick Crogan, *Gameplay Mode: War, Simulation, and Technoculture*, Electronic Mediations 36 (Minneapolis: University of Minnesota Press, 2011), xiv, xiii.

60. Paul N. Edwards, *The Closed World: Computers and the Politics of Discourse in Cold War America*, Inside Technology (Cambridge, MA: MIT, 1997), 12.

61. Peter Galison, "The Ontology of the Enemy: Norbert Wiener and the Cybernetic Vision," *Critical Inquiry* 21, no. 1 (Autumn 1994): 265.

62. David H. Ahl and Robert Leedom, "Super Star Trek," in *The Best of Creative Computing*, ed. David H. Ahl, vol. 1 (Morristown, N.J.: Creative Computing Press, 1976), 275–281. Some sources state earlier release dates for *Star Trek*; see Alexander Smith, *They Create Worlds: The Story of the People and Companies That Shaped the Video Game Industry* (Boca Raton, FL: CRC Press, 2020).

63. Les Levidow and Kevin Robins, eds., *Cyborg Worlds: The Military Information Society* (London: Free Association Books, 1989), 159.

64. McKenzie Wark, *Gamer Theory* (Cambridge, MA: Harvard University Press, 2007), 23.

65. Espen Aarseth, "Doors and Perception: Fiction vs. Simulation in Games," *Intermédialités: Histoire et théorie des arts, des lettres et des techniques*, no. 9 (Spring 2007): 37, https://doi.org/10.7202/1005528ar.

66. Martin Gardner, "Mathematical Games," *Scientific American* 223, no. 4 (October 1970): 120–123.

67. Jon McCormack and Alan Dorin, "Art, Emergence and the Computational Sublime," in *Proceedings of Second Iteration: A Conference on Generative Systems in the Electronic Arts* (Melbourne: CEMA, 2001), 78.

68. Jeffrey Sconce, *Haunted Media: Electronic Presence from Telegraphy to Television*, Console-Ing Passions (Durham, NC: Duke University Press, 2000).

69. For a discussion of ghosts and spectral beings in video games, see Justyna Janik, "Ghosts of the Present Past: Spectrality in the Video Game Object," *Journal of the Philosophy of Games* 2, no. 1 (December 2019), https://doi.org/10.5617/jpg.2943.

70. Fred R. Shapiro, "Etymology of the Computer Bug: History and Folklore," *American Speech* 62, no. 4 (Winter 1987): 376, https://doi .org/10.2307/455415.

71. Anatoly Liberman, "Bugs: An Etymological Postscript," *OUPblog*, June 3, 2015, https://blog.oup.com/2015/06/bug-etymology-word -origin/.

72. Olga Goriunova and Alexei Shulgin, "Glitch," in *Software Studies: A Lexicon*, ed. Matthew Fuller, Leonardo Books (Cambridge, MA: MIT Press, 2008), 110–119.

73. Richard C. Clark, " 'Gremlin' Twenty Years Later," *American Speech* 39, no. 3 (October 1964): 237–239, https://doi.org/10.2307/453638.

74. For an overview of media representation of demons in the traditional sense, see Frans Mäyrä, *Demonic Texts and Textual Demons: The Demonic Tradition, the Self, and Popular Fiction*, Tampere Studies in Literature and Textuality (Tampere, Finland: Tampere University Press, 1999).

75. Jimena Canales and Markus Krajewski, "Little Helpers: About Demons, Angels and Other Servants," *Interdisciplinary Science Reviews* 37, no. 4 (December 2012): 314–331, https://doi.org/10.1179/0308018812Z .00000000025.

76. Canales and Krajewski, 315.

77. Canales and Krajewski, 320.

78. Within video games, Janet Murray has noted that daemons were implemented in the 1977 text adventure *Zork* to "make some things happen automatically without the player's explicit action." Murray, *Hamlet on the Holodeck*, 78.

79. Another similar metaphor, *sprite*, refers to a movable 2D graphic of an object or a creature. The term was coined by the designers of the Texas Instruments TMS9918 video controller chip to describe the almost supernatural ease with which these images can fly across the screen. Jeff White, "Karl Guttag Conference on Delphi TI Net," post on comp.sys .ti Google Group February 11, 1993, https://groups.google.com/g/comp .sys.ti/c/QlLThkrm8Po/m/GtnkyhtF4nMJ.

80. *Doom* (id Software, 1993), PC.

CHAPTER 2

1. Lord British, *Akalabeth* (California Pacific Computer Company, 1980), Apple II.

2. Gerard Jones, *Killing Monsters: Why Children Need Fantasy, Super Heroes, and Make-Believe Violence* (New York: Basic Books, 2002).

3. Simon Egenfeldt-Nielsen, Jonas Heide Smith, and Susana Pajares Tosca, *Understanding Video Games: The Essential Introduction*, 3rd ed. (New York: Routledge, 2015), 268. Tanya Krzywinska points out that monsters "present a threat but also endorse a sense of a player's agency through their death." Tanya Krzywinska, "Gothic American Gaming," in *The Cambridge Companion to American Gothic*, ed. Jeffrey Andrew Weinstock (Cambridge: Cambridge University Press, 2017), 233.

4. Staffan Björk and Jussi Holopainen, *Patterns in Game Design*, Charles River Media Game Development Series (Hingham, MA: Charles River Media, 2005), 70.

5. If we consider snakes to be monsters, then the game snakes and ladders is an exception. In its original Indian versions, snakes represent human vices and "the spiritual defilements which hinder the soul in its . . . upward journey." Andrew Topsfield, "The Indian Game of Snakes and Ladders," *Artibus Asiae* 46, no. 3 (1985): 207, https://doi.org/10.2307/3250203. Also, some versions of the game of the goose represented their playing fields as serpents. Marjolein Leesberg, "The Royal Game of Cupid: A 17th-Century Board Game," British Library: Picturing Places, accessed August 21, 2021, https://www.bl.uk/picturing-places/articles/the-royal-game-of-cupid-a-17th-century-board-game.

6. Based on an Internet Archive query made on January 10, 2022.

7. Chris Elgood, *Handbook of Management Games*, 5th ed. (Aldershot, UK: Gower, 1993), 11.

8. According to Richard Bartle (personal communication), players of MUD used the expression "player vs. player" already in the early 1990s. Based on a Google Group query made on January 11, 2022, the earliest preserved mentions of "player vs. environment" or "PvE" appeared in December 1998 on a USENET newsgroup dedicated the *Ultima Online* and *EverQuest* MMORPGs. Silverlock, "Again where did you . . . ,"

comment on rec.games.computer.ultima.online Google Group post
"Raph has it wrong . . . The Mage tower is not PK friendly!!!", December
4, 1998, https://groups.google.com/g/rec.games.computer.ultima.online
/c/QVd8iPtxs-M/m/ew-Pu497eyMJ; Rob, "Cross post from EQVault
Board," post on alt.games.everquest Google Group, December 22, 1998,
https://groups.google.com/g/alt.games.everquest/c/XIKjYc6LrqY/m
/xVRlUbphjRQJ.

9. Melissa Tyler, *Dark Age of Camelot: Prima's Official Strategy Guide*,
rev. ed. (Roseville, CA: Prima Games, 2002), 397.

10. Alenda Y. Chang similarly describes player versus environment
as the type of play where "the focus is on completing game objectives
and progressing against nonplayer characters, for instance, by slaying
monsters." Alenda Y. Chang, *Playing Nature: Ecology in Video Games*,
Electronic Mediations 58 (Minneapolis: University of Minnesota
Press, 2019), 199.

11. Naughty Dog, *The Last of Us* (Sony Computer Entertainment,
2013), PS3; *The Witcher 3: Wild Hunt* (CD Projekt, 2015), PC.

12. *League of Legends* (Riot Games, 2009), PC.

13. It only mentions "extra-individual" interaction patterns in games
like solitaire, where the player interacts with passive objects. Elliott M.
Avedon, "The Structural Elements of Games," in *The Study of Games*,
ed. Elliott M. Avedon and Brian Sutton-Smith (New York: John Wiley
& Sons, 1971), 419–426.

14. Jim Dunnigan, *Outdoor Survival* (Baltimore: Avalon Hill, 1972).
D&D's outdoor campaigns were inspired by *Outdoor Survival* and
expected the players to own a copy of it.

15. Devin Monnens and Martin Goldberg, "Space Odyssey: The
Long Journey of Spacewar! from MIT to Computer Labs Around the
World," in "Cultural History of Video Games," special issue, *Kinepha-
nos* 5 (June 2015): 124–147.

16. *The Oregon Trail* (Don Rawitsch, Bill Heinemann, and Paul Dil-
lenberger, 1971), HP 2100; David H. Ahl and Robert Leedom, "Super
Star Trek," in *The Best of Creative Computing*, ed. David H. Ahl, vol. 1
(Morristown, N.J.: Creative Computing Press, 1976), 275–281.

17. Esther MacCallum-Stewart, Jaakko Stenros, and Staffan Björk, "The Impact of Role-Playing Games on Culture," in *Role-Playing Game Studies: Transmedia Foundations*, ed. José P. Zagal and Sebastian Deterding (New York: Routledge, 2018), 172–187.

18. Jon Peterson, *The Elusive Shift: How Role-Playing Games Forged Their Identity*, Game Histories (Cambridge, MA: MIT Press, 2020).

19. Jon Peterson, *Playing at the World: A History of Simulating Wars, People and Fantastic Adventures, from Chess to Role-Playing Games* (San Diego: Unreason Press, 2013), chap. 4.

20. Robert T. Tally, "Demonizing the Enemy, Literally: Tolkien, Orcs, and the Sense of the World Wars," *Humanities* 8, no. 1 (March 2019): 54, https://doi.org/10.3390/h8010054.

21. See also Nicolas LaLone, "A Tale of Dungeons & Dragons and the Origins of the Game Platform," *Analog Game Studies* 6, no. 3 (September 2019), https://analoggamestudies.org/2019/09/a-tale-of-dungeons -dragons-and-the-origins-of-the-game-platform/.

22. Peterson, *Playing at the World*, 157.

23. Gary Gygax and Dave Arneson, *Dungeon & Dragons Volume 2: Monsters & Treasure* (Lake Geneva, WI: Tactical Studies Rules, 1974); Gary Gygax, *Advanced Dungeons & Dragons: Monster Manual* (Lake Geneva, WI: TSR Games, 1979).

24. Sarah Stang and Aaron Trammell, "The Ludic Bestiary: Misogynistic Tropes of Female Monstrosity in *Dungeons & Dragons*," *Games and Culture* 15, no. 6 (2020): 735, https://doi.org/10.1177/1555412019850059.

25. Hit chance and damage were initially calculated from hit points before becoming independent stats.

26. Gygax and Arneson, *Dungeon & Dragons Volume 2*, 12–13.

27. Espen Aarseth, "Doors and Perception: Fiction vs. Simulation in Games," *Intermédialités: Histoire et théorie des arts, des lettres et des techniques*, no. 9 (Spring 2007): 34–44, https://doi.org/10.7202/1005528ar.

28. Gygax, *Advanced Dungeons & Dragons: Monster Manual*, 5.

29. Matt Horrigan, "Aggregate Monsters: Ecologies Challenging Encounters," in "The Friend Folio," special issue, *Analog Game Studies* 8 (October 2021), https://analoggamestudies.org/2021/10/aggregate -monsters-ecologies-challenging-encounters/.

30. According to the 1974 rules, elves and dwarves could not, however, reach the highest character levels available to humans.

31. Gary Gygax, *Advanced Dungeons & Dragons: Dungeon Masters Guide* (Lake Geneva, WI: TSR Games, 1979), 21.

32. Stang and Trammell, "The Ludic Bestiary," 733.

33. Antero Garcia, "Privilege, Power, and Dungeons & Dragons: How Systems Shape Racial and Gender Identities in Tabletop Role-Playing Games," *Mind, Culture, and Activity* 24, no. 3 (July 2017): 232–246, https://doi.org/10.1080/10749039.2017.1293691.

34. Gary Gygax, *Dungeon Module D3: Vault of the Drow* (Lake Geneva, WI: TSR Games, 1978), 23.

35. Matthew Chrulew, "'Masters of the Wild': Animals and the Environment in Dungeons & Dragons," *Concentric: Literary and Cultural Studies* 32, no. 1 (January 2006): 137.

36. For more about extinction (and the absence of it) in video games, see Erik van Ooijen, "On the Brink of Virtual Extinction: Hunting and Killing Animals in Open World Video Games," *Eludamos. Journal for Computer Game Culture* 9, no. 1 (September 2018): 33–45.

37. For more about the virtualization of gameplay objects, demonstrated by the example of shooting gallery targets, see Michael Cowan, "Interactive Media and Imperial Subjects: Excavating the Cinematic Shooting Gallery," *NECSUS*, July 18, 2018, https://necsus-ejms.org /interactive-media-and-imperial-subjects-excavating-the-cinematic -shooting-gallery/.

38. The offshoot *D&D Miniatures Game*, published between 2003 and 2011, was a multiplayer collectible miniature tactics game that— unlike the classic *D&D* role-playing game—required all miniatures to be present on the playing field. By default, the player was expected to own all the individual miniatures they would use in battle.

39. Chrulew, " 'Masters of the Wild'," 142.

40. Robert Kuntz and James Ward, *Gods, Demi-Gods & Deities*, Dungeons & Dragons, Supplement IV (Lake Geneva, WI: TSR Games, 1976).

41. Tony DiTerlizzi, "Owlbears, Rust Monsters and Bulettes, Oh My!," *Tony DiTerlizzi: Artist, Author, Wordbuilder* (blog), December 23, 2013, http://diterlizzi.com/essay/owlbears-rust-monsters-and-bulettes-oh-my/.

42. Tracy Hickman and Laura Hickman, *Ravenloft*, Advanced Dungeons & Dragons (Lake Geneva, WI: TSR, 1983).

43. Mayfair Games, *Monsters of Myth & Legend*, Role Aids (Chicago: Mayfair Games, 1984); Aaron Trammell, "How Dungeons & Dragons Appropriated the Orient," *Analog Game Studies* 3, no. 1 (January 2016), http://analoggamestudies.org/2016/01/how-dungeons-dragons -appropriated-the-orient/.

44. Jeff Pimper and Steve Perrin, *All the Worlds' Monsters* (Albany, CA: Chaosium, 1977), sec. Introduction.

45. Gygax, *Advanced Dungeons & Dragons: Monster Manual.*

46. Tim Snider, *Weird Works: Tome of Creatures Offbeat and Downright Strange* (Mansfield, OH: TWS Hobbies, 1983). Handwritten booklet kept at the Strong Museum of Play, PlagMADA papers, no. 1306.

47. Peterson, *Playing at the World.*

48. For an early occurrence of the expression "hack-and-slash" as a genre label, see Deirdre L. Maloy, "The Swordthrust Series: A Survey," *Computer Gaming World* 2, no. 1 (January 1982): 12.

49. *Akalabeth.* The quote (with "hi-res" capitalized as "Hi-Res") comes from the packaging of the game's original, self-published version. For a scanned image, see Jimmy Maher, "Akalabeth," *The Digital Antiquarian* (blog), December 18, 2011, https://www.filfre.net/2011/12 /akalabeth/. Some sources previously indicated a 1979 release date, but 1980 has since been confirmed by Richard Garriott himself; see Jimmy Maher, "A Word on Akalabeth and Chronology," *The Digital Antiquarian* (blog), December 2, 2011, https://www.filfre.net/2011/12 /a-word-on-akalabeth-and-chronology/.

50. *Wizardry: Proving Grounds of the Mad Overlord* (Sir-Tech, 1981), Apple II.

51. Richard A. Bartle, *Designing Virtual Worlds* (Indianapolis: New Riders Publishing, 2004). Additional information from personal email communication with Richard A. Bartle.

52. MUSE, "Mobile," MUDspeke Index, updated September 23, 1999, https://mud.co.uk/muse/mobile.htm.

53. T. L. Taylor, *Play Between Worlds: Exploring Online Game Culture* (Cambridge, MA: MIT Press, 2009).

54. Erkki Huhtamo, "Slots of Fun, Slots of Trouble: An Archaeology of Arcade Gaming," in *Handbook of Computer Game Studies*, ed. Joost Raessens and Jeffrey H. Goldstein (Cambridge, MA: MIT Press, 2005), 3–22.

55. Cowan, "Interactive Media and Imperial Subjects."

56. Richard Tucker and Valerie Tucker, *Step Right up! Classic American Target and Arcade Forms* (Atglen, PA: Schiffer Publishing Ltd, 2014).

57. *Monster Gun* (Midway, 1967), arcade.

58. *Invaders from the Outer Space (The Invaders)* (Midway, 1970), arcade.

59. *Invaders (SEGA Invaders)* (Sega, 1972), arcade; *Monster Gun* (Sega, 1972), arcade.

60. An exception is *Boothill* (1977, Japanese title *Gunman*), which features a shooting duel between two cowboys, one of whom could be controlled by the computer. Although the player-controlled avatar can get shot in the game, I do not consider *Boothill* a player vs. environment game because the computer simulates a human opponent. The game is a sequel to Nishikado's own *Gun Fight* (1975, Japanese title *Western Gun*), which did not feature the one-player option. Both games were designed at Taito and adapted for the North American market by Midway.

61. Bob Rehak, "Playing at Being: Psychoanalysis and the Avatar," in *The Video Game Theory Reader*, ed. Mark J. P. Wolf and Bernard Perron (New York: Routledge, 2003), 114.

62. *Breakout* (Atari, 1976), arcade; *Pong*, (Atari, 1972), arcade.

63. Retro Gamer, "Nishikado-San Speaks," *Retro Gamer* 1, no. 3 (2004): 35.

64. Edge, "Q&A: Tomohiro Nishikado," *Edge* 13, no. 154 (October 2005): 108.

65. Interestingly, though, Nishikado had previously made *Gunfight* (1975). This suggests that a one-on-one duel might not have been considered as problematic as shooting enemies in large quantities.

66. Rachael Hutchinson, *Japanese Culture through Videogames*, Contemporary Japan Series (New York: Routledge, 2019).

67. Edge, "Q&A: Tomohiro Nishikado."

68. Martin Amis, *Invasion of the Space Invaders: An Addict's Guide to Battle Tactics, Big Scores and the Best Machines* (London: Jonathan Cape, 2018), 16.

69. Amis, 47. Italics retained from the original.

70. Raiford Guins, *Atari Design: Impressions on Coin-Operated Video Game Machines*, Cultural Histories of Design (London: Bloomsbury Visual Arts, 2020).

71. *Asteroids* (Atari, 1979), arcade; *Centipede* (Atari, 1981), arcade; *Defender* (Williams Electronics, 1981), arcade; *Galaga* (Namco, 1981), arcade.

72. Matthew Smith, *Manic Miner* (Software Projects, 1983), ZX Spectrum. Quote from the game's cassette inlay.

73. *Super Mario Bros.* (Nintendo, 1985), SNES; *Rayman* (Ubi Soft, 1995), PC.

74. Toru Iwatani, afterword to *The Pac-Man Principle: A User's Guide to Capitalism*, by Alex Wade (Winchester, UK: Zer0 Books, 2018), 74.

75. Alex Wade, *The Pac-Man Principle: A User's Guide to Capitalism* (Winchester, UK: Zer0 Books, 2018), 10.

76. Malcolm Evans and J. K. Greye, *3D Monster Maze* (J. K. Greye Software, 1982), ZX81.

77. Bernard Perron, ed., "Introduction: Gaming After Dark," in *Horror Video Games: Essays on the Fusion of Fear and Play* (Jefferson, NC: McFarland & Co, 2009), 6.

78. In contemporary game design, stealth and avoidance mechanics are mostly used in combination with player vs. environment gameplay. In some scenarios of *Resident Evil 2*, for example, an indestructible creature known as Mr. X stalks the protagonists around the game world, but the game also features destructible zombies. See Bernard Perron, *The World of Scary Video Games: A Study in Videoludic Horror* (New York: Bloomsbury Academic, 2018): 345, 384.

79. MacCallum-Stewart, Stenros, and Björk, "The Impact of Role-Playing Games on Culture," 184.

80. BioWare, *Baldur's Gate* (Interplay, 1998), PC.

81. For a chronicle of the evolution of computer role-playing game mechanics, see Matt Barton, *Dungeons and Desktops: The History of Computer Role-Playing Games* (Wellesley, MA: A K Peters, 2008).

82. Krzywinska, "Gothic American Gaming," 233.

83. Epic Games, *Gears of War* (Microsoft Game Studios, 2006), Xbox 360.

84. *Gauntlet* (Atari, 1985), arcade.

85. *Gauntlet: Monsters and Players Preface*, collection of Strong Museum of Play, Atari Coin-Op Division corporate records, item no. 114.6238, box 2, folder 1.

86. Chang, *Playing Nature*, 200.

87. Ulrich Beck, "Individualism," in *The Wiley-Blackwell Encyclopedia of Globalization*, ed. George Ritzer (Chichester, UK: John Wiley & Sons, Ltd, 2012), https://doi.org/10.1002/9780470670590.wbeog292.

88. Krzywinska, "Gothic American Gaming," 232.

89. Braxton Soderman, *Against Flow: Video Games and the Flowing Subject* (Cambridge, MA: MIT Press, 2021), 61. For an earlier critique of the concept, see Brian Schrank, *Avant-Garde Videogames: Playing with Technoculture* (Cambridge, MA: MIT Press, 2014).

90. Soderman, 58.

91. Riccardo Fassone, *Every Game Is an Island: Endings and Extremities in Video Games* (New York: Bloomsbury Academic, 2017), 117.

92. *Diablo* (Blizzard Entertainment, 1997), PC.

93. Mortensen and Jørgensen, *The Paradox of Transgression*, 185. They build on the work by Brian Schrank and Eugénie Shinkle; see Schrank, *Avant-Garde Videogames*; Eugénie Shinkle, "Videogames and the Digital Sublime," in *Digital Cultures and the Politics of Emotion: Feelings, Affect and Technological Change*, ed. Athina Karatzogianni and Adi Kuntsman (London: Palgrave Macmillan UK, 2012), 94–108, https://doi.org/10.1057/9780230391345_6.

94. Perron notes that in horror films, there are "generally more victims than there are monsters," but horror games "turn the equation around." He also mentions that "games with only one killer are 'deviant'" even among survival horror games. Perron, *The World of Scary Video Games*, 369, 384.

95. Georgia Leigh McGregor, "Situations of Play: Patterns of Spatial Use in Videogames," in *Situated Play, Proceedings of DiGRA 2007 Conference* (Digital Games Research Association, 2007), http://www.digra.org/wp-content/uploads/digital-library/07312.05363.pdf.

96. Gary Gygax and Dave Arneson, *Dungeon & Dragons Volume 3: The Underworld & Wilderness Adventures* (Lake Geneva, WI: Tactical Studies Rules, 1974), 14.

97. René Glas, "Of Heroes and Henchmen: The Conventions of Killing Generic Expendables in Digital Games," in *The Dark Side of Game Play: Controversial Issues in Playful Environments*, ed. Torill Elvira Mortensen, Jonas Linderoth, and Ashley M. L Brown (London: Routledge, 2015), 33–49; Nathan Hunt, "A Utilitarian Antagonist: The Zombie in Popular Video Games," in *The Zombie Renaissance in Popular Culture*, ed. Laura Hubner, Marcus Leaning, and Paul Manning (London: Palgrave Macmillan UK, 2015), 107–123, https://doi.org/10.1057/9781137276506_8.

98. Stainless Games, *Carmaggedon* (Sales Curve Interactive, 1997), PC.

99. Carly A. Kocurek, "Who Hearkens to the Monster's Scream? Death, Violence and the Veil of the Monstrous in Video Games," *Visual Studies* 30, no. 1 (January 2015): 79–89, https://doi.org/10.1080/1472586X .2015.996402.

100. Jaroslav Švelch, "Always Already Monsters—'*BioShock*"s (2007) 'Splicers' as Computational Others," *Nordlit*, no. 42 (November 2019), https://doi.org/10.7557/13.5015.

101. *BioShock* (2K Games, 2007), PC; *Deathloop* (Bethesda Softworks, 2021), PS5. There is also a practical reason for using masks: they may save the labor of designing unique and realistic faces.

102. Björk and Holopainen, *Patterns in Game Design*, 70. For the sake of readability, I have removed capitalization of key terms.

103. Naughty Dog, *The Last of Us*; *The Last of Us Part II* (Sony Interactive Entertainment, 2020), PS4.

104. For a discussion of differentiation among zombies, see: Hunt, "A Utilitarian Antagonist."

105. I discuss fungibility in more detail in Švelch, "Always Already Monsters."

106. Clara Fernández-Vara, "Dracula Defanged: Empowering the Player in Castlevania: Symphony of the Night," *Loading . . .* 4, no. 6 (2010): 7.

107. Roger Luckhurst, *Zombies: A Cultural History* (London: Reaktion Books, 2015), 173.

CHAPTER 3

1. Kazunori Inoue, "On Creating Enemies," *PlatinumGames Official Blog*, October 16, 2009, https://www.platinumgames.com/official-blog /article/1924.

2. Martin Robinson, *The Art of Dead Space* (London: Titan Books, 2013), 83.

3. Paige V. Polinsky, *Pokémon Designer: Satoshi Tajiri*, Toy Trailblazers (Minneapolis: Abdo Publishing, 2017).

4. Santa Monica Studio, *God of War* (Sony Interactive Entertainment, 2018), PS4.

5. Olli Sotamaa and Jan Švelch, eds., *Game Production Studies* (Amsterdam: Amsterdam University Press, 2021), https://doi.org/10.5117/9789463725439. For more about paratextuality, see Jan Švelch, "Paratextuality in Game Studies: A Theoretical Review and Citation Analysis," *Game Studies* 20, no. 2 (June 2020), http://gamestudies.org/2002/articles/jan_svelch.

6. David Wengrow, "Gods and Monsters: Image and Cognition in Neolithic Societies," *Paléorient* 37, no. 1 (2011): 153–163.

7. David Wengrow, *The Origins of Monsters: Image and Cognition in the First Age of Mechanical Reproduction*, The Rostovtzeff Lectures (Princeton: Princeton University Press, 2014), 73.

8. Wengrow, *Origins of Monsters*.

9. Already in the first century BC, the Roman architect Vitruvius dismissed monster imagery as nonsensical, frivolous, and indicative of "depraved taste," complaining that "monsters are now painted in frescoes rather than reliable images of definite things." Marcus Vitruvius Pollio, *Vitruvius: Ten Books on Architecture*, trans. Ingrid D. Rowland (New York: Cambridge University Press, 1999), 91.

10. This kind of imagination was, however, rarely unleashed in the medieval bestiaries, which drew on a limited stock of visual templates that were either copied from existing sources or from collections maintained by illumination workshops. Xenia Muratova, "Workshop Methods in English Late Twelfth-Century Illumination and the Production of Luxury Bestiaries," in *Beasts and Birds of the Middle Ages*, ed. Willene B. Clark and Meredith T. McMunn (Philadelphia: University of Pennsylvania Press, 1989), 53–68, https://doi.org/10.9783/9781512805512-005.

11. Michael Camille, *Image on the Edge: The Margins of Medieval Art*, Essays in Art and Culture (London: Reaktion Books, 2010), 12.

12. Michael Camille, *The Gargoyles of Notre-Dame: Medievalism and the Monsters of Modernity* (Chicago: University of Chicago Press, 2009), 17. As was the case of manuscript illuminators, masons who sculpted

these gargoyles tended to be lay professionals who worked from their own designs, which did not necessarily conform to the expectations of the church. Camille, *Image on the Edge*.

13. Camille, *Image on the Edge*, 65.

14. Kirk Ambrose, *The Marvellous and the Monstrous in the Sculpture of Twelfth-Century Europe*, Boydell Studies in Medieval Art and Architecture (Woodbridge, UK: Boydell Press, 2013), 6.

15. Michael Squire, "'Fantasies so Varied and Bizarre': The Domus Aurea, the Renaissance, and the 'Grotesque,'" in *A Companion to the Neronian Age*, ed. Emma Buckley and Martin T. Dinter (Oxford, UK: Wiley-Blackwell, 2013), 444–464, https://doi.org/10.1002/9781 118316771.ch25.

16. Squire, 450.

17. M. M. Bakhtin, *Rabelais and His World* (Bloomington: Indiana University Press, 1984), 63.

18. Both quotes: Camille, *Gargoyles of Notre-Dame*, 26.

19. Stuart Husband, "It Came from Los Angeles," *Guardian*, December 18, 1999, http://www.theguardian.com/books/1999/dec/18/books.guar dianreview7; Don Chaffey, dir., *Jason and the Argonauts* (Columbia Pictures, 1963); Desmond Davis, dir., *Clash of the Titans* (United Artists, 1981).

20. Manuel Ferri Gandía, "Influences of the Animator Ray Harryhausen in the Design of Fantastic Creatures for Videogames," in *In a Stranger Field. Studies of Art, Audiovisuals and New Technologies in Fantasy, SciFi and Horror Genres*, ed. Mario-Paul Martínez and Fran Mateu (Elche, Spain: Association for Development and Dissemination of the Fantastic Genre "Black Unicorn," 2019). *Golden Axe* (Sega, 1989), arcade.

21. Nathan H. Juran, dir., *The 7th Voyage of Sinbad* (Columbia Pictures, 1958).

22. Julie A. Turnock, *Plastic Reality: Special Effects, Technology, and the Emergence of 1970s Blockbuster Aesthetics*, Film and Culture (New York: Columbia University Press, 2015), 243.

23. Jason Weiser, "Episode 6—The Sundering of Jötunheim," *The Lost Pages of Norse Myth*, February 27, 2018, podcast, sec. 13:08–13:25, https://open.spotify.com/show/3fiW5OG2ry4NHGB0wmANVI; Capcom, "The Making of *Monster Hunter: World*—Part Three: Craft," Monster Hunter, February 7, 2018, YouTube video, sec. 1:20–1:55, https://www.youtube.com/watch?v=Eo9j1-E2k3I.

24. Gunther R Kress and Theo Van Leeuwen, *Reading Images: The Grammar by Visual Design* (London: Routledge, 1996), 158–159.

25. Camille, *Gargoyles of Notre-Dame*, 149.

26. Wengrow, *Origins of Monsters*.

27. Leonardo da Vinci, *Notebooks*, ed. Irma A. Richter and Thereza Wells, Oxford World's Classics (Oxford: Oxford University Press, 2008), 160.

28. Husband, "It Came from Los Angeles."

29. Margrit Shildrick, "Visual Rhetorics and the Seductions of the Monstrous: Some Precautionary Observations," *Somatechnics* 8, no. 2 (September 2018): 167, https://doi.org/10.3366/soma.2018.0248.

30. Mark Lamoureux, "8-Bit Primitive: Homage to the Atari 2600," in *Gamers: Writers, Artists & Programmers on the Pleasure of Pixels*, ed. Shana Compton (New York: Soft Skull Press, 2004), 82–83; *Phoenix* (Atari, 1983), Atari 2600; *Demon Attack* (Imagic, 1982), Atari 2600.

31. See chapter 2 for more details and references.

32. John Romero, "Cyberdemon model scan, circa 1993," Twitter, December 10, 2014, https://twitter.com/romero/status/542616760789127170; David Kushner, *Masters of Doom: How Two Guys Created an Empire and Transformed Pop Culture* (New York: Random House, 2004).

33. Tanya Krzywinska, "Zombies in Gamespace: Form, Context, and Meaning in Zombie-Based Video Games," in *Zombie Culture: Autopsies of the Living Dead*, ed. Shawn McIntosh and Marc Leverette (Lanham, MD: Scarecrow Press, 2008), 157.

34. Santa Monica Studio, "Making of—*God of War* (2005) [Behind the Scenes]," NeoGamer—The Video Game Archive, uploaded 2020,

YouTube video, 13:24, https://www.youtube.com/watch?v=VHdbIy E3A24&ab_channel=NeoGamer-TheVideoGameArchive.

35. *Devil May Cry* (Capcom, 2001), PS2.

36. Rob Gallagher, "Minecrafting Masculinities: Gamer Dads, Queer Childhoods and Father-Son Gameplay in A Boy Made of Blocks," *Game Studies* 18, no. 2 (September 2018), http://gamestudies.org/1802 /articles/gallagher.

37. Barlog was also involved in minute details such as envisioning that the Valkyries would "wear a harness of metal wings rather than natural feathered wings." Evan Shamoon, ed., *The Art of God of War* (Milwaukie, OR: Dark Horse Books, 2018), 142.

38. Shamoon, 30.

39. PlayStation, "*God of War*'s Bestiary: The Troll | Countdown to Launch," PlayStation, April 17, 2018, YouTube video, 1:43, https:// www.youtube.com/watch?v=AVDWOiYXpv0.

40. When I defeated a Troll by the name of Járn Fótr in my play-through of *God of War*, I watched him tumble to the ground—then, about a second later, several pieces of shiny loot unceremoniously popped out of his corpse. Although I happily accepted them, I found this scene rather jarring. The drive for "mythical realism" was side-lined to make the reward clearly visible to the player. To me, it disgraced the Troll and undermined the labor of writers and artists who aimed to create a majestic, awe-inspiring creature.

41. Jason Weiser, "Episode 2—And Only Rage Remained," *The Lost Pages of Norse Myth*, September 27, 2017, Podcast, 37:50, https://open .spotify.com/show/3fiW5OG2ry4NHGB0wmANVI.

42. Denny Yeh, "How Santa Monica Studio Created God of War's Greatest Challenge," *PlayStation.Blog*, February 1, 2019, https://blog .playstation.com/2019/02/01/how-santa-monica-studio-created-god -of-wars-greatest-challenge/.

43. Santa Monica Studio, "God of War," PlayStation.com, accessed June 20, 2018, https://godofwar.playstation.com/stories/deconstructing -hr%C3%A6zlyr.

44. Daniel Birczyński, "DD2018: Daniel Birczyński—The Sound of *God of War*, 2018," Digital Dragons, July 6, 2018, YouTube video, 51:57, https://www.youtube.com/watch?v=hPvjGC3CHdA&ab_channel =DigitalDragons.

45. *Monster Hunter: World* (Capcom, 2018), PS4.

46. Andrew Webster, "How New Technology Helped Make Monster Hunter World's Beasts Even More Terrifying," *Verge*, February 1, 2018, https://www.theverge.com/2018/2/1/16955336/monster-hunter -world-creature-design-interview.

47. 2K Boston, *BioShock* (2K Games, 2007), PC.

48. I have discussed the monster design of *BioShock* at length in Jaroslav Švelch, "Always Already Monsters—'*BioShock*"s (2007) 'Splicers' as Computational Others," *Nordlit*, no. 42 (November 2019), https:// doi.org/10.7557/13.5015.

49. Gamasutra Staff, "Take a Look at Some of the Earliest Designs for Plants vs. Zombies," *Gamasutra*, May 6, 2019, https://www.gamasutra .com/view/news/342128/Take_a_look_at_some_of_the_earliest_ designs_for_Plants_vs_Zombies.php.

50. Matthew Barr, "Zombies, Again? A Qualitative Analysis of the Zombie Antagonist's Appeal in Game Design," in *The Playful Undead and Video Games*, ed. Stephen J. Webley and Peter Zackariasson (New York: Routledge, 2019), 15–29. Barr quotes from an interview with Chris Avellone, a writer and designer who worked on the *Fallout* series, among other titles.

51. Thomas Grip and Olof Strand, "Amnesia: The Dark Descent: Birth of a Monster—Part 2," *Gamasutra*, March 18, 2011, https://www .gamedeveloper.com/art/amnesia-the-dark-descent-birth-of-a-monster ---part-2-.

52. Sychov Brothers, "Skeleton Lightweight," Unreal Engine [Marketplace], November 6, 2019, https://www.unrealengine.com /marketplace/en-US/product/skeleton-lightweight/reviews.

53. Dirk Pellett, "Open Letter to ClassicGaming.Com," Dirk Pellet's WWW Home Page, updated April 28, 2006, http://www.armory.com /~dlp/dnd1.html.

54. *Phoenix* (Taito, 1980), arcade.

55. *Xevious* (Namco, 1982), arcade; see Tristan Donovan, *Replay: The History of Video Games* (East Sussex, UK: Yellow Ant, 2010).

56. *Super Mario Bros.* (Nintendo, 1985), SNES; *The Legend of Zelda* (Nintendo, 1987), Nintendo Entertainment System.

57. Clive Thompson, "Who's the Boss?," *Wired*, May 8, 2006, https://web.archive.org/web/20080508192019/http:/www.wired.com/gaming/gamingreviews/commentary/games/2006/05/70832.

58. Game Informer Staff, "Our Full Hidetaka Miyazaki Sekiro: Shadows Die Twice Interview," *Game Informer*, January 25, 2019, https://www.gameinformer.com/2019/01/25/our-full-hidetaka-miyazaki-sekiro-shadows-die-twice-interview.

59. Wil Murray, ed., *Bloodborne Collector's Edition Guide* (Hamburg: Future Press, 2015), 544.

60. Thompson, "Who's the Boss?"

61. Stephen T. Asma, *On Monsters: An Unnatural History of Our Worst Fears* (Oxford: Oxford University Press, 2012), 192.

62. Michael McWhertor, "Hidetaka Miyazaki on Dark Souls 3's Changes to Bosses, Magic, Combat and More," *Polygon*, August 10, 2015, https://www.polygon.com/2015/8/10/9115299/dark-souls-3-hidetaka-miyazaki-interview-gamescom.

63. Andrew Wood and Adam Summerville, "Understanding Boss Battles: A Case Study of Cuphead," paper presented at the *AIIDE Workshop on Experimental AI in Games 2019*, http://www.exag.org/archive/wood2019battles.pdf.

64. Yeh, "How Santa Monica Studio Created God of War's Greatest Challenge."

65. Thompson, "Who's the Boss?"

66. I have discussed the process of learning about monsters in more detail in a study of *Alien: Isolation.* Jaroslav Švelch, "Should the Monster Play Fair?: Reception of Artificial Intelligence in *Alien: Isolation*," *Game Studies* 20, no. 2 (June 2020), http://gamestudies.org/2002/articles/jaroslav_svelch.

67. Thompson, "Who's the Boss?"

68. Jaroslav Švelch, "Monsters by the Numbers: Controlling Monstrosity in Video Games," in *Monster Culture in the 21st Century: A Reader*, ed. Marina Levina and Diem-My T Bui (New York: Bloomsbury Academic, 2013), 193–208.

69. Wesley Yin-Poole, "Deus Ex Boss Battles Outsourced," *Eurogamer*, September 19, 2011, https://www.eurogamer.net/articles/2011-09-19 -deus-ex-boss-battles-outsourced.

70. Donovan, *Replay*, 117.

71. Yeh, "How Santa Monica Studio Created God of War's Greatest Challenge."

72. Georgios N. Yannakakis and Julian Togelius, *Artificial Intelligence and Games* (Cham, Switzerland: Springer International Publishing, 2018).

73. Švelch, "Should the Monster Play Fair?"

74. Brenda Garno, *Wizardry VI: Bane of the Cosmic Forge Playmaster's Compendium* (Sir-Tech, 1991), 19.

75. Turnock, *Plastic Reality*.

76. Michaël Samyn, "Bayonetta and the Vatican," *Notgames Blog*, April 27, 2010, https://web.archive.org/web/20100610203419/http:// notgames.org/blog/2010/04/27/bayonetta-and-the-vatican/; Platinum Games, *Bayonetta* (Sega, 2009), PS3.

77. Inoue, "On Creating Enemies."

78. Inoue.

79. Weiser, "And Only Rage Remained." The remaining 20 percent reportedly consist of *keyframe* animation. In keyframe animation, the animator specifies locations or properties of certain elements (such as joints) at certain frames of the animation sequence, leaving animation software to automatically interpolate the frames in between to create a smooth transition.

80. Axel Grossman, "Santa Monica Studio Presents: *God of War*—GDC Autodesk Developer Day Sessions." Autodesk Media and Entertainment,

April 15, 2019, Vimeo video, 1:06:27, https://vimeo.com/330507722. The technique of adapting animation data to another character is called *retargeting*.

81. Alex Avard and 2020, "The Making of a Rat King: How Naughty Dog Created Its Scariest Foe in The Last of Us Part 2," GamesRadar+, October 16, 2020, https://www.gamesradar.com/the-last-of-us-2-rat -king-making-of/.

82. Capcom, "The Making of *Monster Hunter*."

83. Krzywinska, "Zombies in Gamespace."

CHAPTER 4

1. *Undertale* (Toby Fox, 2015), PC.

2. Paul J. Crutzen, "Geology of Mankind," *Nature* 415, no. 23 (January 2002), https://doi.org/10.1038/415023a.

3. Bruno Latour, *Reset Modernity!: The Field Book*, ed. Bruno Latour et al. (Karlsruhe: ZKM Center for Art and Media, 2016), C–5.

4. For example, see Judith Butler, *Gender Trouble: Feminism and the Subversion of Identity* (New York: Routledge, 1990); Judith Halberstam, *The Queer Art of Failure* (Durham, NC: Duke University Press, 2011); Leela Gandhi, *Postcolonial Theory: A Critical Introduction* (Sydney: Allen & Unwin, 2014); Human Animal Research Network Editorial Collective, ed., *Animals in the Anthropocene: Critical Perspectives on Non-Human Futures*, Animal Publics (Sydney: Sydney University Press, 2015).

5. Patricia MacCormack, "Posthuman Teratology," in *The Ashgate Research Companion to Monsters and the Monstrous*, ed. Asa Simon Mittman and Peter Dendle, Ashgate Research Companions (Farnham, UK: Ashgate, 2013), 295.

6. Jeffrey Andrew Weinstock, "Invisible Monsters: Vision, Horror, and Contemporary Culture," in *The Ashgate Research Companion to Monsters and the Monstrous*, ed. Asa Simon Mittman and Peter Dendle, Ashgate Research Companions (Farnham, UK: Ashgate, 2013), 276.

7. Weinstock, "Invisible Monsters."

8. Line Henriksen, Morten Hillgaard Bülow, and Erika Kvistad, "Monstrous Encounters: Feminist Theory and the Monstrous," *Women, Gender & Research* 26, no. 2–3 (2017): 5.

9. Roger Luckhurst, "After Monster Theory?: Gareth Edwards's *Monsters*," *Science Fiction Film & Television* 13, no. 2 (July 2020): 278–279, https://doi.org/10.3828/sfftv.2020.14; Steffen Hantke, "The State of the State of Emergency: Life under Alien Occupation in Gareth Edwards' 'Monsters,'" *AAA: Arbeiten Aus Anglistik Und Amerikanistik* 41, no. 1 (2016): 25–38.

10. Matt Reeves, dir., *Cloverfield* (Paramount Pictures, 2008).

11. Gareth Edwards, dir., *Monsters* (Vertigo Films, 2010).

12. Luckhurst, "After Monster Theory?," 285.

13. Peter Galison, "The Ontology of the Enemy: Norbert Wiener and the Cybernetic Vision," *Critical Inquiry* 21, no. 1 (Autumn 1994). See chapter 2 of this book.

14. Jordan Mechner, *Prince of Persia* (Brøderbund Software, 1989), Apple II.

15. Jordan Mechner, *The Making of Prince of Persia: Journals, 1985–1993* (South San Francisco: Stripe Press, 2020).

16. For a detailed discussion of doubles in video games, see Laurie N. Taylor, "Not of Woman Born: Monstrous Interfaces and Monstrosity in Video Games," PhD diss. (University of Florida, 2006), 70–74, https://ufdc.ufl.edu/UFE0013427/00001.

17. The Grue, along with the messages cited, already appears in the source code of the 1977 mainframe version archived at MIT. Zork source code, 1977, MIT Tapes of Tech Square (ToTS) collection, MC-0741. MIT Department of Distinctive Collections, Cambridge, MA, https://archivesspace.mit.edu/repositories/2/archival_objects/347748. The word "Grue" was likely borrowed from Jack Vance's *Dying Earth* fantasy series, although Vance used it to describe a different creature—see Jack Vance, *The Eyes of the Overworld* (New York: Ace Books, 1966).

18. Daniel Fandino, "Grues," in *100 Greatest Video Game Characters*, ed. Jaime Banks, Robert Mejia, and Aubrie Adams (Lanham, MD: Rowman & Littlefield Publishers, 2017), 68.

19. According to Fandino, the Grue "became an iconic element of Info-com games and of the golden age of interactive fiction." Fandino, 68.

20. J. R. R. Tolkien, "Beowulf: The Monsters and the Critics," in *The Monsters and the Critics and Other Essays*, ed. Christopher Tolkien (London: HarperCollins, 1997), 33.

21. Tolkien, 26.

22. Tolkien, 23.

23. Stephen T. Asma, *On Monsters: An Unnatural History of Our Worst Fears* (Oxford: Oxford University Press, 2012), 99.

24. Tolkien, "Beowulf," 31.

25. Tanya Krzywinska, "The Gamification of Gothic Coordinates in Videogames," *Revenant* 1, no. 1 (2015): 58–78.

26. Team Ico, *Shadow of the Colossus* (Sony Computer Entertainment, 2005), PS2; Nick Fortugno, "Losing Your Grip: Futility and Dramatic Necessity in Shadow of the Colossus," in *Well Played 1.0: Video Games, Value and Meaning*, ed. Drew Davidson (Pittsburgh: ETC Press, 2009), 171–188; Miguel Sicart, *The Ethics of Computer Games* (Cambridge, MA: MIT Press, 2009).

27. Kristan Reed, "Interview of the Colossus," *Eurogamer*, November 10, 2005, https://www.eurogamer.net/articles/i_sotc_ps2.

28. Kikizo Staff, "Shadow of the Colossus: Exclusive New Interview, All-New Trailer & Screens," *Kikizo Archives*, March 21, 2005, http://archive.videogamesdaily.com/features/shadowofthecolossus_inter-view_march05.asp.

29. Jay Taylor, "Interview Extra: Fumito Ueda (Ico, Shadow of the Colossus, The Last Guardian)," *Cane and Rinse*, August 27, 2019, https://caneandrinse.com/fumito-ueda-interview/.

30. For a discussion of music in *Shadows of the Colossus*, see Tom Cole, "The Tragedy of Betrayal: How the Design of Ico and Shadow of the Colossus Elicits Emotion," in *Proceedings of the 2015 DiGRA International Conference* (Digital Games Research Association, 2015), http://www.digra.org/wp-content/uploads/digital-library/189_Cole_The-Tragedy-of-Betrayal.pdf.

31. Taylor, "Interview Extra."

32. Miguel César, *Transgressing Death in Japanese Popular Culture* (Cham, Switzerland: Palgrave Macmillan, 2020), 101, https://doi.org /10.1007/978-3-030-50880-7.

33. César, 121.

34. Before *Shadow of the Colossus*, the ethical aspects of heroism were explored in computer role-playing games, notably in the *Ultima* series. See Andrew Black, "Lord British's Ethics—Interrogating Virtue in the Ultima: Age of Enlightenment Series," *The Computer Games Journal* 6, no. 3 (September 2017): 113–133, https://doi.org/10.1007/s40869-017 -0034-7.

35. FromSoftware, *Dark Souls: Design Works* (Richmond Hill, ON: UDON Entertainment, 2013), 115.

36. Aphorism no. 146. Friedrich Wilhelm Nietzsche, *Beyond Good and Evil: Prelude to a Philosophy of the Future*, ed. Rolf-Peter Horstmann and Judith Norman, Cambridge Texts in the History of Philosophy (Cambridge: Cambridge University Press, 2002), 69.

37. 2K Boston, *BioShock* (2K Games, 2007), PC; Yager Development, *Spec Ops: The Line* (2K Games, 2012), PC.

38. *God of War* (Sony Interactive Entertainment, 2018), PS4.

39. *Undertale*.

40. Steven Bogos, "Undertale Dev: 'Every Monster Should Feel Like an Individual,'" *The Escapist*, June 25, 2013, https://www.escapistmagazine .com/v2/undertale-dev-every-monster-should-feel-like-an-individual/.

41. *Shin Megami Tensei* (Atlus, 1992), SNES.

42. Bonnie Ruberg, "Straight-Washing 'Undertale': Video Games and the Limits of LGBTQ Representation," *Transformative Works and Cultures* 28 (September 2018), para. 2.4, https://doi.org/10.3983/twc .2018.1516.

43. *Ultima VI: The False Prophet* (Origin Systems, 1990), PC. See Black, "Lord British's Ethics."

44. See also Jaroslav Švelch, "The Good, the Bad, and the Player: The Challenges to Moral Engagement in Single-Player Avatar-Based Video Games," in *Ethics and Game Design: Teaching Values through Play*, ed. Karen Schrier and David Gibson (Hershey, PA: Information Science Reference, 2010), 52–68.

45. *The Witcher 3: Wild Hunt* (CD Projekt, 2015), PC.

46. Monolith Productions, *Middle-Earth: Shadow of Mordor* (WB Games, 2014), PC; *Middle-Earth: Shadow of War* (WB Games, 2017), PC.

47. Robert T. Tally, "Demonizing the Enemy, Literally: Tolkien, Orcs, and the Sense of the World Wars," *Humanities* 8, no. 1 (March 2019): 54, https://doi.org/10.3390/h8010054. References to Orcs as a "race" appear already in Tolkien's fiction, not only in later interpretations.

48. Matt Purslow, "Developers, Why Aren't You Using the Nemesis System? Making a Case for the Generation's Best New Mechanic," *PCGamesN*, March 30, 2017, https://www.pcgamesn.com/middle-earth -shadow-of-war/shadow-of-mordor-nemesis-system-clones.

49. Ben Kuchera, "*Shadow of Mordor*'s Nemesis System Is Simpler than You Think, and Should Be Stolen," *Polygon*, October 13, 2014, https:// www.polygon.com/2014/10/13/6970533/shadow-of-mordors-nemesis -system-is-simpler-than-you-think-and-should; Purslow, "Developers."

50. Michael de Plater et al., Nemesis Characters, Nemesis Forts, Social Vendettas and Followers in Computer Games, US Patent US20160279522A1, filed March 25, 2016, published September 29, 2016, and granted February 23, 2021, https://patents.google.com/patent /US20160279522A1/en.

51. Marianne Gunderson, "Other Ethics: Decentering the Human in Weird Horror," *Women, Gender & Research*, no. 2–3 (November 2017): 13, https://doi.org/10.7146/kkf.v26i2-3.110547.

52. Daniel Vella, "No Mastery Without Mystery: Dark Souls and the Ludic Sublime," *Game Studies* 15, no. 1 (July 2015), http://gamestudies .org/1501/articles/vella.

53. Justyna Janik, "The Material World of Digital Fictions," *Images: The International Journal of European Film, Performing Arts and Audiovisual*

Communication 29, no. 38 (June 2021): 70, https://doi.org/10.14746/i
.2021.38.04.

54. *Amnesia: The Dark Descent* (Frictional Games, 2010), PC; Bernard
Perron, *The World of Scary Video Games: A Study in Videoludic Horror* (New
York: Bloomsbury Academic, 2018): 345, 384; Hart, *Monstrous Forms*.

55. Sandy Petersen, *Call of Cthulhu* (Oakland: Chaosium, 1981); *Eternal Darkness: Sanity's Requiem* (Nintendo, 2002), Nintendo GameCube.

56. smartalic5, "Amnesia Water Monster 360 [Lurker]," August 8, 2011,
YouTube video, 0:56, https://www.youtube.com/watch?v=32Jbvw
-Fm0U.

57. Adam Charles Hart, *Monstrous Forms: Moving Image Horror across
Media* (New York: Oxford University Press, 2020), 166.

58. *Control* (505 Games, 2019), PC.

59. Future Press, *The Art and Making of Control Limited Edition* (Hamburg: Future Press, 2020), 181.

60. Another notable kind of deceptive monster is the shapeshifter.
A whole family of video game shapeshifters has been inspired by the
Mimics from *D&D* and can take on the appearance of a common
chest (as in the *Dark Souls* series), or morph into office furniture (as
in the 2017 sci-fi action game *Prey*). *Dark Souls* (Namco Bandai, 2011),
PS3; *Prey* (Bethesda Softworks, 2017), PC.

61. Alexander R. Galloway and Eugene Thacker, *The Exploit: A Theory
of Networks*, Electronic Mediations 21 (Minneapolis: University of
Minnesota Press, 2007), 5.

62. See chapter 1.

63. Matthew J. Weise, "How the Zombie Changed Videogames," in
Zombies Are Us: Essays on the Humanity of the Walking Dead, ed. Christopher M. Moreman and Cory Rushton (Jefferson, NC: McFarland,
2011), 163. Although this observation was made in 2011, it still holds.

64. Exceptions include the mainstream survival action game *ZombiU*
and the independent survival simulation *Project Zomboid*. *ZombiU*,

(Ubisoft, 2012), Wii U; *Project Zomboid [Early Access Version]* (The Indie Stone, 2013), PC.

65. Eric T. Lofgren and Nina H. Fefferman, "The Untapped Potential of Virtual Game Worlds to Shed Light on Real World Epidemics," *The Lancet Infectious Diseases* 7, no. 9 (September 2007): 625–629, https://doi.org/10.1016/S1473-3099(07)70212-8.

66. Manuel DeLanda, *Philosophy and Simulation: The Emergence of Synthetic Reason* (London: Continuum, 2011), 1.

67. Jesper Juul, *Half-Real: Video Games Between Real Rules and Fictional Worlds* (Cambridge, MA: MIT Press, 2005).

68. *Dead Rising* (Capcom, 2006), Xbox 360. The quote appeared on the back of the European boxed version.

69. See also Kristine Jørgensen, "*Dead Rising* and the Gameworld Zombie," in *The Playful Undead and Video Games*, ed. Stephen J. Webley and Peter Zackariasson (New York: Routledge, 2019), 126–137.

70. Matthew J. Weise, "The Rules of Horror: Procedural Adaptation in *Clock Tower*, *Resident Evil*, and *Dead Rising*," in *Horror Video Games: Essays on the Fusion of Fear and Play*, ed. Bernard Perron (Jefferson, NC: McFarland & Co, 2009), 258.

71. Galloway and Thacker, *Exploit*, 66.

72. BioWare, *Mass Effect 3* (Electronic Arts, 2012), PC; The Coalition, *Gears 5* (Xbox Game Studios, 2019), PC. For a discussion of aggregate monsters in *D&D*, see Matt Horrigan, "Aggregate Monsters: Ecologies Challenging Encounters," in "The Friend Folio," special issue, *Analog Game Studies* 8 (October 2021), https://analoggamestudies.org/2021/10/aggregate-monsters-ecologies-challenging-encounters/.

73. Alex Wiltshire, "How A Plague Tale: Innocence's Rat Hordes Were Made," *Rock Paper Shotgun*, December 18, 2019, https://www.rockpapershotgun.com/how-a-plague-tale-innocences-rat-hordes-were-made.

74. James O'Sullivan, "Collective Consciousness in Science Fiction," *Foundation* 39, no. 110 (Winter 2010): 80–85.

75. David "Zeb" Cook, *Planescape Campaign Setting: Monstrous Supplement* (Lake Geneva, WI: TSR, 1994), 9.

76. Mike Mearls, ed., *Dungeons & Dragons: Volo's Guide to Monsters* (Renton, WA: Wizards of the Coast, 2016), 133.

77. Black Isle Studios, *Planescape: Torment* (Interplay, 1999), PC.

78. Eugénie Shinkle, "Videogames and the Digital Sublime," in *Digital Cultures and the Politics of Emotion: Feelings, Affect and Technological Change*, ed. Athina Karatzogianni and Adi Kuntsman (London: Palgrave Macmillan UK, 2012), 94–108, https://doi.org/10.1057/9780230 391345_6.

79. *Metal Gear Solid* (Konami, 1998), Sony PlayStation.

80. Marty Sliva, "Top 100 Unforgettable Video Game Moments," IGN, accessed July 19, 2021, https://www.ign.com/lists/top-100-video-game -moments.

81. Stephanie Boluk and Patrick LeMieux, *Metagaming: Playing, Competing, Spectating, Cheating, Trading, Making, and Breaking Videogames*, Electronic Mediations 53 (Minneapolis: University of Minnesota Press, 2017), 143.

82. Steven Conway, "A Circular Wall? Reformulating the Fourth Wall for Videogames," *Journal of Gaming & Virtual Worlds* 2, no. 2 (August 2010): 151, https://doi.org/10.1386/jgvw.2.2.145_1.

83. Toby Fox, *Undertale: Art Book* (Fangamer, 2016), 140.

84. The expansion of the fourth wall is taken even further by the 2017 title *Doki Doki Literature Club*. While superficially following the conventions of the visual novel genre, the game changes after the death of one of the characters. At that point, the game is subject to recurring glitches and narrative breakdowns. The death is later revealed to be the doing of the game's villain, who can only be defeated by deleting her character file from the game's data folder. *Doki Doki Literature Club* (Team Salvato, 2017), PC.

85. While discussing the fourth wall phenomenon, Jørgensen notes that it is common for games to directly address the player through

their interface. Moments described in this section, however, break the conventions of how the interface is used in the rest of the game. Kristine Jørgensen, *Gameworld Interfaces* (Cambridge, MA: MIT Press, 2013), 124–126.

86. Creative Assembly, *Alien: Isolation* (Sega, 2014), PC. The analysis of the game presented here draws from my previously published work; see Jaroslav Švelch, "Should the Monster Play Fair?: Reception of Artificial Intelligence in *Alien: Isolation*," *Game Studies* 20, no. 2 (June 2020), http://gamestudies.org/2002/articles/jaroslav_svelch.

87. Creative Assembly, "*Alien: Isolation* Developer Diary—'Creating The Alien' [International]," Alien: Isolation, March 13, 2014, YouTube video, sec. 0:52–0:55, https://www.youtube.com/watch?v=6W6OpHB2D4Q.

88. Creative Assembly, sec. 2:06–2:15.

89. Tommy Thompson, "The Perfect Organism," *Becoming Human*, April 24, 2017, https://becominghuman.ai/the-perfect-organism-d350 c05d8960.

90. Švelch, "Should the Monster Play Fair?"

91. Brendan Keogh and Darshana Jayemanne, "'Game Over, Man. Game Over': Looking at the Alien in Film and Videogames," *Arts* 7, no. 3 (August 2018): 43, https://doi.org/10.3390/arts7030043.

92. Arthur Gies, "Alien Isolation Review: Crew Expendable," *Polygon*, October 3, 2014, https://www.polygon.com/2014/10/3/6142209/alien -isolation-review-xbox-one-PS4; dFUSE, "You'll Be Surprised How Few Gamers Actually Finished Alien: Isolation," *PlayStation Mania*, January 29, 2015, https://www.psmania.net/2015/01/youll-be-surprised-how -few-gamers-actually-finished-alien-isolation-was-the-game-too-well -made.

93. *No Man's Sky* (Hello Games, 2016), PC.

94. Rebellion Developments, *Aliens vs. Predator* (Sega, 2010), PC.

95. Thomas Nagel, "What Is It Like to Be a Bat?," *The Philosophical Review* 83, no. 4 (October 1974): 435–450, https://doi.org/10.2307 /2183914. For a discussion of portraying bat-ness in games, see Stefano

Gualeni, "What Is It Like to Be a (Digital) Bat?," paper presented at the Philosophy of Computer Games Conference 2011, Athens, https://gua -le-ni.com/articles/Digital_Bat.pdf.

96. Jonne Arjoranta, "Playing the Nonhuman: Alien Experiences in Aliens vs. Predator," in *Reconfiguring Human, Nonhuman and Posthuman in Literature and Culture*, ed. Sanna Karkulehto, Aino-Kaisa Koistinen, and Essi Varis, Perspectives on the Non-Human in Literature and Culture (New York: Routledge, 2019), 121. Playing as demons and monstrous characters has been also explored by Mäyrä; see Frans Mäyrä, "From the Demonic Tradition to Art-Evil in Digital Games: Monstrous Pleasures in Lord of the Rings Online," in *Ringbearers: The Lord of the Rings Online as Intertextual Narrative*, ed. Tanya Krzywinska, Esther MacCallum-Stewart, and Justin Parsler (Manchester: Manchester University Press, 2011), 111–135.

97. Phobia Game Studio, *Carrion* (Devolver Digital, 2020), PC.

98. Aphra Kerr, *Global Games: Production, Circulation and Policy in the Networked Era* (London: Routledge/Taylor & Francis Group, 2017).

CONCLUSION

1. Ridley Scott, dir., *Alien* (20th Century Fox, 1979).

2. Jeffrey Jerome Cohen, "Monster Culture (Seven Theses)," in *Monster Theory: Reading Culture*, ed. Jeffrey Jerome Cohen (Minneapolis: University of Minnesota Press, 1996); Patricia MacCormack, "Posthuman Teratology," in *The Ashgate Research Companion to Monsters and the Monstrous*, ed. Asa Simon Mittman and Peter Dendle, Ashgate Research Companions (Farnham, UK: Ashgate, 2013).

3. For a critique of gamification, see Ian Bogost, "Why Gamification Is Bullshit," in *The Gameful World: Approaches, Issues, Applications*, ed. Steffen P. Walz and Sebastian Deterding (Cambridge, MA: MIT Press, 2014), 65–79.

4. Clara Fernández-Vara, "Dracula Defanged: Empowering the Player in Castlevania: Symphony of the Night," *Loading . . .* 4, no. 6 (2010), http://journals.sfu.ca/loading/index.php/loading/article/view /88; Roger Luckhurst, *Zombies: A Cultural History* (London: Reaktion

Books, 2015); Aaron Trammell, "How *Dungeons & Dragons* Appropriated the Orient," *Analog Game Studies* 3, no. 1 (January 2016), http://analoggamestudies.org/2016/01/how-dungeons-dragons-appropriated-the-orient/; Sarah Stang, "The Broodmother as Monstrous-Feminine—Abject Maternity in Video Games," *Nordlit*, no. 42 (November 2019): 233–256, https://doi.org/10.7557/13.5014; Sarah Stang and Aaron Trammell, "The Ludic Bestiary: Misogynistic Tropes of Female Monstrosity in *Dungeons & Dragons*," *Games and Culture* 15, no. 6 (2020): 735, https://doi.org/10.1177/1555412019850059.

5. Eric N. Bailey, Kazunori Miyata, and Tetsuhiko Yoshida, "Gender Composition of Teams and Studios in Video Game Development," *Games and Culture* 16, no. 1 (January 2021): 42–64, https://doi.org/10.1177/1555412019868381.

6. Likewise, the popular Japanese survival horror series *Resident Evil* was a direct response to the 1992 French game *Alone in the Dark*, adopting both its cinematic camerawork and its resilient monsters. Carl Therrien, "Games of Fear: A Multi-Faceted Historical Account of the Horror Genre in Video Games," in *Horror Video Games: Essays on the Fusion of Fear and Play*, ed. Bernard Perron (Jefferson, NC: McFarland & Co, 2009), 26–45; *Alone in the Dark* (Infogrames, 1992), PC.

7. *The Witcher 3: Wild Hunt* (CD Projekt, 2015), PC; Morteshka, *Black Book* (HypeTrain Digital, 2021), PC.

8. *Nightfall: Escape* (Zeenoh Inc., 2016), PC; Christoffer Mitch C. Cerda, "Playing Horrific History: Philippine Mythological and Folk Creatures and the Trauma of Colonial History in the Design and Narrative of Nightfall: Escape," paper presented at the 18th Annual Tampere University Game Research Lab Spring Seminar, Tempere, Finland, 2021.

9. Michael Dylan Foster, "Early Modern Past to Postmodern Future: Changing Discourses of Japanese Monsters," in *The Ashgate Research Companion to Monsters and the Monstrous*, ed. Asa Simon Mittman and Peter Dendle, Ashgate Research Companions (Farnham, UK: Ashgate, 2013), 133–150.

10. For a (journalistic) critique of *Monster Hunter*, see: Dia Lacina, "Monster Hunter World Can't Envision That Maybe Hunters Are the

Baddies," *Paste Magazine*, February 28, 2019, https://www.pastemagazine
.com/games/monster-hunter-world/monster-hunter-world-cant
-envision-that-maybe-hunt/.

11. The list would be even longer if one counted diminutives, such as *potvůrka*, *příšerka*, or *zrůdička*.

12. *Kingdom Death: Monster* (Kingdom Death, 2015), tabletop; Mike Elliot and Jonathan Tweet, *Hecatomb* (Wizards of the Coast, 2005), tabletop.

13. Tampere University Game Research Lab, "Monstrosity—The 17th Annual Tampere University Game Research Lab Spring Seminar," Tampere University of Applied Sciences, https://www.tuni.fi/en/news /monstrosity-17th-annual-tampere-university-game-research-lab -spring-seminar. References to individual presentations are included throughout the book.

14. Don Turnbull, ed., *Advanced Dungeons & Dragons: Fiend Folio* (Lake Geneva, WI: TSR Games, 1981).

15. Wesley Yin-Poole, "Single-Player Games 'Gone in 3 Years,'" *Eurogamer*, August 16, 2011, https://www.eurogamer.net/articles/2011-08 -16-single-player-only-games-gone-in-3-years; Dave Thier, "Yes, AAA Single-Player Games Are Dying, And That's Fine," *Forbes*, October 18, 2017, https://www.forbes.com/sites/davidthier/2017/10/18/star-wars -visceral-yes-aaa-single-player-games-are-dying-thats-fine/.

16. Tyler Wilde, "The Live Service Gold Rush Hasn't Stopped Single-player Games from Thriving," *PC Gamer*, March 18, 2021, https:// www.pcgamer.com/singleplayer-games-live-service/.

17. *Fortnite* (Epic Games, 2017), PC; *League of Legends* (Riot Games, 2009), PC.

18. Alenda Y. Chang, *Playing Nature: Ecology in Video Games*, Electronic Mediations 58 (Minneapolis: University of Minnesota Press, 2019), 199.

19. Chang, 201. Italics adjusted.

BIBLIOGRAPHY

2K Boston. *BioShock*. PC. 2K Games, 2007.

Aarseth, Espen. "Doors and Perception: Fiction vs. Simulation in Games." *Intermédialités: Histoire et théorie des arts, des lettres et des techniques*, no. 9 (Spring 2007): 35–44. https://doi.org/10.7202/1005528ar.

Ahl, David H., and Robert Leedom. "Super Star Trek." In *The Best of Creative Computing*, edited by David H. Ahl, 1:275–281. Morristown, NJ: Creative Computing Press, 1976.

Allison, Anne. *Millennial Monsters: Japanese Toys and the Global Imagination*. Berkeley: University of California Press, 2006.

Ambrose, Kirk. *The Marvellous and the Monstrous in the Sculpture of Twelfth-Century Europe*. Boydell Studies in Medieval Art and Architecture. Woodbridge, UK: Boydell Press, 2013.

Amis, Martin. *Invasion of the Space Invaders: An Addict's Guide to Battle Tactics, Big Scores and the Best Machines*. London: Jonathan Cape, 2018.

Amstar Electronics. *Phoenix*. Atari 2600. Atari, 1983.

Arjoranta, Jonne. "Playing the Nonhuman: Alien Experiences in Aliens vs. Predator." In *Reconfiguring Human, Nonhuman and Posthuman in Literature and Culture*, edited by Sanna Karkulehto, Aino-Kaisa Koistinen, and Essi Varis, 108–124. Perspectives on the Non-Human in Literature and Culture. New York: Routledge, 2019.

Arkane Studios. *Deathloop*. PS5. Bethesda Softworks, 2021.

———. *Prey*. PC. Bethesda Softworks, 2017.

Asma, Stephen T. *On Monsters: An Unnatural History of Our Worst Fears*. Oxford: Oxford University Press, 2012.

Atari. *Asteroids*. Arcade. Atari, 1979.

———. *Breakout*. Arcade. Atari, 1976.

———. *Centipede*. Arcade. Atari, 1981.

———. *Gauntlet*. Arcade. Atari, 1985.

———. *Pong*. Arcade. Atari, 1972.

Atlus. *Shin Megami Tensei*. SNES. Atlus, 1992.

Avard, Alex. "The Making of a Rat King: How Naughty Dog Created Its Scariest Foe in The Last of Us Part 2." *GamesRadar+*, October 16, 2020. https://www.gamesradar.com/the-last-of-us-2-rat-king-making-of/.

Avedon, Elliott M. "The Structural Elements of Games." In *The Study of Games*, edited by Elliott M. Avedon and Brian Sutton-Smith, 419–426. New York: John Wiley & Sons, 1971.

Azuma, Hiroki. *Otaku: Japan's Database Animals*. English ed. Minneapolis: University of Minnesota Press, 2009.

Backe, Hans-Joachim, and Espen J. Aarseth. "Ludic Zombies: An Examination of Zombieism in Games." In *Proceedings of the 2013 DiGRA International Conference: DeFragging Game Studies*. Digital Games Research Association, 2013. http://www.digra.org/wp-content/uploads/digital-library/paper_405.pdf.

Bailey, Eric N., Kazunori Miyata, and Tetsuhiko Yoshida. "Gender Composition of Teams and Studios in Video Game Development." *Games and Culture* 16, no. 1 (January 2021): 42–64. https://doi.org/10.1177/1555412019868381.

Bakhtin, M. M. *Rabelais and His World*. Bloomington: Indiana University Press, 1984.

Barr, Matthew. "Zombies, Again? A Qualitative Analysis of the Zombie Antagonist's Appeal in Game Design." In *The Playful Undead and Video Games*, edited by Stephen J. Webley and Peter Zackariasson, 15–29. New York: Routledge, 2019.

Bartle, Richard A. *Designing Virtual Worlds*. Indianapolis: New Riders Publishing, 2004.

Barton, Matt. *Dungeons and Desktops: The History of Computer Role-Playing Games*. Wellesley, MA: A K Peters, 2008.

Beal, Timothy K. *Religion and Its Monsters*. New York: Routledge, 2002.

Beck, Ulrich. "Individualism." In *The Wiley-Blackwell Encyclopedia of Globalization*, edited by George Ritzer. Chichester, UK: John Wiley & Sons, Ltd, 2012. https://doi.org/10.1002/9780470670590.wbeog292.

———. "World Risk Society and Manufactured Uncertainties." *Iris. European Journal of Philosophy and Public Debate* 1, no. 2 (2009): 291–299. https://www.torrossa.com/en/resources/an/2489448.

BioWare. *Baldur's Gate*. PC. Interplay, 1998.

———. *Mass Effect 3*. PC. Electronic Arts, 2012.

Birczyński, Daniel. "DD2018: Daniel Birczyński—The Sound of *God of War*, 2018." Digital Dragons, July 6, 2018. YouTube video, 51:57. https://www.youtube.com/watch?v=hPvjGC3CHdA&ab_channel =DigitalDragons.

Björk, Staffan, and Jussi Holopainen. *Patterns in Game Design*. Charles River Media Game Development Series. Hingham, MA: Charles River Media, 2005.

Black, Andrew. "Lord British's Ethics—Interrogating Virtue in the Ultima: Age of Enlightenment Series." *The Computer Games Journal* 6, no. 3 (September 2017): 113–133. https://doi.org/10.1007/s40869 -017-0034-7.

Black Isle Studios. *Planescape: Torment*. PC. Interplay, 1999.

Blizzard North. *Diablo*. PC. Blizzard Entertainment, 1997.

Bogos, Steven. "Undertale Dev: 'Every Monster Should Feel Like an Individual.'" *The Escapist*, June 25, 2013. https://www.escapistmagazine .com/v2/undertale-dev-every-monster-should-feel-like-an-individual/.

Bogost, Ian. "Why Gamification Is Bullshit." In *The Gameful World: Approaches, Issues, Applications*, edited by Steffen P. Walz and Sebastian Deterding, 65–79. Cambridge, MA: MIT Press, 2014.

Boluk, Stephanie, and Patrick LeMieux. *Metagaming: Playing, Competing, Spectating, Cheating, Trading, Making, and Breaking Videogames*. Electronic Mediations 53. Minneapolis: University of Minnesota Press, 2017.

Butler, Judith. *Gender Trouble: Feminism and the Subversion of Identity*. New York: Routledge, 1990.

Caillois, Roger. *Man, Play, and Games*. Urbana: University of Illinois Press, 2001.

Camille, Michael. *Image on the Edge: The Margins of Medieval Art*. Essays in Art and Culture. London: Reaktion Books, 2010.

———. *The Gargoyles of Notre-Dame: Medievalism and the Monsters of Modernity*. Chicago: University of Chicago Press, 2009.

Campbell, Joseph. *The Hero with a Thousand Faces*. Commemorative ed. Bollingen Series 17. Princeton, NJ: Princeton University Press, 2004.

Canales, Jimena, and Markus Krajewski. "Little Helpers: About Demons, Angels and Other Servants." *Interdisciplinary Science Reviews* 37, no. 4 (December 2012): 314–331. https://doi.org/10.1179/0308018812Z.00000000025.

Capcom. *Dead Rising*. Xbox 360. Capcom, 2006.

———. "The Making of Monster Hunter: World—Part Three: Craft." Monster Hunter, February 7, 2018. YouTube video: 7:20. https://www.youtube.com/watch?v=Eo9j1-E2k3I.

———. *Monster Hunter: World*. PS4. Capcom, 2018.

Capcom. *Devil May Cry*. PS2. Capcom, 2001.

Carr, Diane. "Textual Analysis, Digital Games, Zombies." In *Proceedings of the 2009 DiGRA International Conference: Breaking New Ground: Innovation in Games, Play, Practice and Theory*. Digital Games Research Association, 2009. http://www.digra.org/wp-content/uploads/digital-library/09287.241711.pdf.

Carroll, Noël. *The Philosophy of Horror: Or, Paradoxes of the Heart*. New York: Routledge, 1990.

CD Projekt RED. *The Witcher 3: Wild Hunt*. PC. CD Projekt, 2015.

Cerda, Christoffer Mitch C. "Playing Horrific History: Philippine Mythological and Folk Creatures and the Trauma of Colonial History in the Design and Narrative of Nightfall: Escape." Paper presented at the 18th Annual Tampere University Game Research Lab Spring Seminar, Tampere, Finland, 2021.

César, Miguel. *Transgressing Death in Japanese Popular Culture*. Cham, Switzerland: Palgrave Macmillan, 2020. https://doi.org/10.1007/978-3-030-50880-7.

Chaffey, Don, dir. *Jason and the Argonauts*. Columbia Pictures, 1963.

Chang, Alenda Y. *Playing Nature: Ecology in Video Games*. Electronic Mediations 58. Minneapolis: University of Minnesota Press, 2019.

Chrulew, Matthew. "'Masters of the Wild': Animals and the Environment in Dungeons & Dragons." *Concentric: Literary and Cultural Studies* 32, no. 1 (January 2006): 135–168.

Clark, Richard C. "'Gremlin' Twenty Years Later." *American Speech* 39, no. 3 (October 1964): 237–239. https://doi.org/10.2307/453638.

Clark, Willene B. *A Medieval Book of Beasts: The Second-Family Bestiary: Commentary, Art, Text and Translation.* Woodbridge, UK: Boydell Press, 2006.

Cohen, Jeffrey Jerome. "Monster Culture (Seven Theses)." In *Monster Theory: Reading Culture*, edited by Jeffrey Jerome Cohen, 3–25. Minneapolis: University of Minnesota Press, 1996.

Cole, Tom. "The Tragedy of Betrayal: How the Design of Ico and Shadow of the Colossus Elicits Emotion." In *Proceedings of the 2015 DiGRA International Conference.* Digital Games Research Association, 2015. http://www.digra.org/wp-content/uploads/digital-library/189 _Cole_The-Tragedy-of-Betrayal.pdf.

Conway, Steven. "A Circular Wall? Reformulating the Fourth Wall for Videogames." *Journal of Gaming & Virtual Worlds* 2, no. 2 (August 2010): 145–155. https://doi.org/10.1386/jgvw.2.2.145_1.

Cook, David "Zeb." *Planescape Campaign Setting: Monstrous Supplement.* Lake Geneva, WI: TSR, 1994.

Cowan, Michael. "Interactive Media and Imperial Subjects: Excavating the Cinematic Shooting Gallery." *NECSUS*, July 18, 2018. https:// necsus-ejms.org/interactive-media-and-imperial-subjects-excavating -the-cinematic-shooting-gallery/.

Creative Assembly. *Alien: Isolation.* PC. Sega, 2014.

———. "Alien: Isolation Developer Diary—'Creating The Alien' [International]." Alien: Isolation, March 13, 2014. YouTube video, 3:22. https://www.youtube.com/watch?v=6W6OpHB2D4Q.

Creed, Barbara. *The Monstrous-Feminine: Film, Feminism, Psychoanalysis.* Popular Fiction Series. London: Routledge, 1993.

Crogan, Patrick. *Gameplay Mode: War, Simulation, and Technoculture.* Electronic Mediations 36. Minneapolis: University of Minnesota Press, 2011.

Crutzen, Paul J. "Geology of Mankind." *Nature* 415, no. 23 (January 2002). https://doi.org/10.1038/415023a.

Dalley, Stephanie, ed. *Myths from Mesopotamia: Creation, the Flood, Gilgamesh, and Others.* Rev. ed. Oxford World's Classics. Oxford: Oxford University Press, 2000.

Davis, Desmond, dir. *Clash of the Titans.* United Artists, 1981.

DeLanda, Manuel. *Philosophy and Simulation: The Emergence of Synthetic Reason.* London: Continuum, 2011.

Dendle, Peter. "Conclusion: Monsters and the Twenty-First Century: The Preternatural in an Age of Scientific Consensus." In *The Ashgate Research Companion to Monsters and the Monstrous,* edited by Asa Simon Mittman and Peter Dendle, 437–448. Ashgate Research Companions. Farnham, UK: Ashgate, 2013.

Derrida, Jacques. "Some Statements and Truisms about Neologisms, Newisms, Postisms, Parasitisms, and Other Small Seismisms." In *The States of "Theory,"* edited by David Carroll. Translated by Anne Tomiche, 63–94. New York: Columbia University Press, 1990.

dFUSE. "You'll Be Surprised How Few Gamers Actually Finished Alien: Isolation." *PlayStation Mania,* January 29, 2015. https://www.psmania.net/2015/01/youll-be-surprised-how-few-gamers-actually-finished-alien-isolation-was-the-game-too-well-made.

DiTerlizzi, Tony. "Owlbears, Rust Monsters and Bulettes, Oh My!" *Tony DiTerlizzi: Artist, Author, Wordbuilder* (blog), December 23, 2013. http://diterlizzi.com/essay/owlbears-rust-monsters-and-bulettes-oh-my/.

Donovan, Tristan. *Replay: The History of Video Games.* East Sussex, UK: Yellow Ant, 2010.

Dunnigan, Jim. *Outdoor Survival.* Baltimore: Avalon Hill, 1972.

Edge. "Q&A: Tomohiro Nishikado." *Edge* 13, no. 154 (October 2005): 108–109.

Edwards, Gareth, dir. *Monsters.* Vertigo Films, 2010.

Edwards, Paul N. *The Closed World: Computers and the Politics of Discourse in Cold War America.* Inside Technology. Cambridge, MA: MIT Press, 1997.

Egenfeldt-Nielsen, Simon, Jonas Heide Smith, and Susana Pajares Tosca. *Understanding Video Games: The Essential Introduction.* 3rd ed. New York: Routledge, 2015.

Elgood, Chris. *Handbook of Management Games.* 5th ed. Aldershot, UK: Gower, 1993.

Elliot, Mike, and Jonathan Tweet. *Hecatomb*. Card game. Wizards of the Coast, 2005.

Epic Games. *Fortnite*. PC. Epic Games, 2017.

———. *Gears of War*. Xbox 360. Microsoft Game Studios, 2006.

Evans, Malcolm, and J. K. Greye. *3D Monster Maze*. ZX81. J. K. Greye Software, 1982.

Fandino, Daniel. "Grues." In *100 Greatest Video Game Characters*, edited by Jaime Banks, Robert Mejia, and Aubrie Adams, 68–70. Lanham, MD: Rowman & Littlefield Publishers, 2017.

Fassone, Riccardo. *Every Game Is an Island: Endings and Extremities in Video Games*. New York: Bloomsbury Academic, 2017.

Fernández-Vara, Clara. "Dracula Defanged: Empowering the Player in Castlevania: Symphony of the Night." *Loading . . .* 4, no. 6 (2010). http://journals.sfu.ca/loading/index.php/loading/article/view/88.

Ferri Gandía, Manuel. "Influences of the Animator Ray Harryhausen in the Design of Fantastic Creatures for Videogames." In *In a Stranger Field. Studies of Art, Audiovisuals and New Technologies in Fantasy, SciFi and Horror Genres*, edited by Mario-Paul Martínez and Fran Mateu. Elche, Spain: Association for Development and Dissemination of the Fantastic Genre "Black Unicorn," 2019.

Ferris, Emil. *My Favorite Thing Is Monsters*. Seattle, WA: Fantagraphics Books, 2017.

Fortugno, Nick. "Losing Your Grip: Futility and Dramatic Necessity in Shadow of the Colossus." In *Well Played 1.0: Video Games, Value and Meaning*, edited by Drew Davidson, 171–188. Pittsburgh: ETC Press, 2009.

Foster, Michael Dylan. "Early Modern Past to Postmodern Future: Changing Discourses of Japanese Monsters." In *The Ashgate Research Companion to Monsters and the Monstrous*, edited by Asa Simon Mittman and Peter Dendle, 133–150. Ashgate Research Companions. Farnham, UK: Ashgate, 2013.

Fox, Toby. *Undertale*. PC. Self-published, 2015.

———. *Undertale: Art Book*. Fangamer, 2016.

Franklin, James. *The Science of Conjecture: Evidence and Probability before Pascal*. Paperback ed. A Johns Hopkins Paperback. Baltimore: Johns Hopkins University Press, 2015.

Frictional Games. *Amnesia: The Dark Descent*. PC. Frictional Games, 2010.

FromSoftware. *Bloodborne*. PS4. Sony Computer Entertainment, 2015.

———. *Dark Souls*. PS3. Namco Bandai, 2011.

———. *Dark Souls: Design Works*. Richmond Hill, ON: Udon Entertainment, 2013.

Future Press. *The Art and Making of Control Limited Edition*. Hamburg: Future Press, 2020.

Galison, Peter. "The Ontology of the Enemy: Norbert Wiener and the Cybernetic Vision." *Critical Inquiry* 21, no. 1 (Autumn 1994): 228–266. https://www.jstor.org/stable/1343893.

Gallagher, Rob. "Minecrafting Masculinities: Gamer Dads, Queer Childhoods and Father-Son Gameplay in A Boy Made of Blocks." *Game Studies* 18, no. 2 (September 2018). http://gamestudies.org/1802/articles/gallagher.

Galloway, Alexander R., and Eugene Thacker. *The Exploit: A Theory of Networks*. Electronic Mediations 21. Minneapolis: University of Minnesota Press, 2007.

Gamasutra Staff. "Take a Look at Some of the Earliest Designs for Plants vs. Zombies." *Gamasutra*, May 6, 2019. https://www.gamasutra.com/view/news/342128/Take_a_look_at_some_of_the_earliest_designs_for_Plants_vs_Zombies.php.

Game Informer Staff. "Our Full Hidetaka Miyazaki Sekiro: Shadows Die Twice Interview." *Game Informer*, January 25, 2019. https://www.gameinformer.com/2019/01/25/our-full-hidetaka-miyazaki-sekiro-shadows-die-twice-interview.

Gandhi, Leela. *Postcolonial Theory: A Critical Introduction*. Sydney: Allen & Unwin, 2014.

Garcia, Antero. "Privilege, Power, and Dungeons & Dragons: How Systems Shape Racial and Gender Identities in Tabletop Role-Playing Games." *Mind, Culture, and Activity* 24, no. 3 (July 2017): 232–246. https://doi.org/10.1080/10749039.2017.1293691.

Gardner, Martin. "Mathematical Games." *Scientific American* 223, no. 4 (October 1970): 120–123.

Garno, Brenda. *Wizardry VI: Bane of the Cosmic Forge Playmaster's Compendium*. Sir-Tech, 1991.

Gies, Arthur. "Alien Isolation Review: Crew Expendable." *Polygon*, October 3, 2014. https://www.polygon.com/2014/10/3/6142209/alien-isolation-review-xbox-one-PS4.

Glas, René. "Of Heroes and Henchmen: The Conventions of Killing Generic Expendables in Digital Games." In *The Dark Side of Game Play: Controversial Issues in Playful Environments*, edited by Torill Elvira Mortensen, Jonas Linderoth, and Ashley M. L Brown, 33–49. London: Routledge, 2015.

Goriunova, Olga, and Alexei Shulgin. "Glitch." In *Software Studies: A Lexicon*, edited by Matthew Fuller, 110–119. Leonardo Books. Cambridge, MA: MIT Press, 2008.

Greenberg, Andrew C., and Robert Woodhead. *Wizardry: Proving Grounds of the Mad Overlord*. Apple II. Sir-Tech, 1981.

Grip, Thomas, and Olof Strand. "Amnesia: The Dark Descent: Birth of a Monster—Part 2." *Gamasutra*, March 18, 2011. https://www.gamedeveloper.com/art/amnesia-the-dark-descent-birth-of-a-monster--part-2-.

Grossman, Axel. "Santa Monica Studio Presents: God of War—GDC Autodesk Developer Day Sessions." Autodesk Media and Entertainment, April 15, 2019. Vimeo video, 1:06:27. https://vimeo.com/330507722.

Gualeni, Stefano. "What Is It Like to Be a (Digital) Bat?" Paper presented at the Philosophy of Computer Games Conference 2011, Athens. https://gua-le-ni.com/articles/Digital_Bat.pdf.

Guins, Raiford. *Atari Design: Impressions on Coin-Operated Video Game Machines*. Cultural Histories of Design. London: Bloomsbury Visual Arts, 2020.

Gunderson, Marianne. "Other Ethics: Decentering the Human in Weird Horror." *Women, Gender & Research*, no. 2–3 (November 2017): 12–24. https://doi.org/10.7146/kkf.v26i2-3.110547.

Gygax, Gary. *Advanced Dungeons & Dragons: Dungeon Masters Guide*. Lake Geneva, WI: TSR Games, 1979.

———. *Advanced Dungeons & Dragons: Monster Manual*. Lake Geneva, WI: TSR Games, 1979.

———. *Dungeon Module D3: Vault of the Drow*. Lake Geneva, WI: TSR Games, 1978.

Gygax, Gary, and Dave Arneson. *Dungeon & Dragons Volume 2: Monsters & Treasure*. Lake Geneva, WI: Tactical Studies Rules, 1974.

———. *Dungeon & Dragons Volume 3: The Underworld & Wilderness Adventures*. Lake Geneva, WI: Tactical Studies Rules, 1974.

Halberstam, Judith. *The Queer Art of Failure*. Durham, NC: Duke University Press, 2011.

Hantke, Steffen. "The State of the State of Emergency: Life under Alien Occupation in Gareth Edwards' 'Monsters.'" *AAA: Arbeiten Aus Anglistik Und Amerikanistik* 41, no. 1 (2016): 25–38.

Haraway, Donna. "The Promises of Monsters: A Regenerative Politics for Inappropriate/d Others." In *Cultural Studies*, edited by Lawrence Grossberg, Cary Nelson, and Paula A. Treichler, 295–336. New York: Routledge, 1992.

Hart, Adam Charles. *Monstrous Forms: Moving Image Horror across Media*. New York: Oxford University Press, 2020.

Hart, Clive. *Kites: An Historical Survey*. Rev. 2nd ed. Mount Vernon, NY: Paul P. Appel, 1982.

Hello Games. *No Man's Sky*. PC. Hello Games, 2016.

Henriksen, Line, Morten Hillgaard Bülow, and Erika Kvistad. "Monstrous Encounters: Feminist Theory and the Monstrous." *Women, Gender & Research* 26, no. 2–3 (2017): 3–11.

Hickman, Tracy, and Laura Hickman. *Ravenloft*. Advanced Dungeons & Dragons. Lake Geneva, WI: TSR, 1983.

Horrigan, Matt. "Aggregate Monsters: Ecologies Challenging Encounters." In "The Fiend Folio." Special issue, *Analog Game Studies* 8 (October 2021). https://analoggamestudies.org/2021/10/aggregate-monsters-ecologies-challenging-encounters/.

Huhtamo, Erkki. "Slots of Fun, Slots of Trouble: An Archaeology of Arcade Gaming." In *Handbook of Computer Game Studies*, edited by Joost Raessens and Jeffrey H. Goldstein, 3–22. Cambridge, MA: MIT Press, 2005.

Huizinga, Johan. *Homo Ludens: A Study of the Play-Element in Culture*. London: Routledge & Kegan Paul, 1949.

Human Animal Research Network Editorial Collective, ed. *Animals in the Anthropocene: Critical Perspectives on Non-Human Futures*. Animal Publics. Sydney: Sydney University Press, 2015.

Hunt, Nathan. "A Utilitarian Antagonist: The Zombie in Popular Video Games." In *The Zombie Renaissance in Popular Culture*, edited by Laura Hubner, Marcus Leaning, and Paul Manning, 107–123. London: Palgrave Macmillan UK, 2015. https://doi.org/10.1057/9781137276506_8.

Husband, Stuart. "It Came from Los Angeles." *Guardian*, December 18, 1999. http://www.theguardian.com/books/1999/dec/18/books.guardianreview7.

Hutchinson, Rachael. *Japanese Culture through Videogames*. Contemporary Japan Series. New York: Routledge, 2019.

id Software. *Doom*. PC. id Software, 1993.

Imagic. *Demon Attack*. Atari 2600. Imagic, 1982.

Infogrames. *Alone in the Dark*. PC. Infogrames, 1992.

Inoue, Kazunori. "On Creating Enemies." *PlatinumGames Official Blog*, October 16, 2009. https://www.platinumgames.com/official-blog/article/1924.

Iwatani, Toru. Afterword to *The Pac-Man Principle: A User's Guide to Capitalism*, by Alex Wade, 74–75. Winchester, UK: Zer0 Books, 2018.

Janik, Justyna. "Ghosts of the Present Past: Spectrality in the Video Game Object." *Journal of the Philosophy of Games* 2, no. 1 (December 2019). https://doi.org/10.5617/jpg.2943.

———. "The Material World of Digital Fictions." *Images: The International Journal of European Film, Performing Arts and Audiovisual Communication* 29, no. 38 (June 2021): 57–72. https://doi.org/10.14746/i.2021.38.04.

Jenkins, Henry. *Comics and Stuff*. New York: New York University Press, 2020.

Jobling, Ian. "The Psychological Foundations of the Hero-Ogre Story: A Cross-Cultural Study." *Human Nature* 12, no. 3 (September 2001): 247–272. https://doi.org/10.1007/s12110-001-1009-7.

Jones, Gerard. *Killing Monsters: Why Children Need Fantasy, Super Heroes, and Make-Believe Violence*. New York: Basic Books, 2002.

Jørgensen, Kristine. "*Dead Rising* and the Gameworld Zombie." In *The Playful Undead and Video Games*, edited by Stephen J. Webley and Peter Zackariasson, 126–137. New York: Routledge, 2019.

———. *Gameworld Interfaces*. Cambridge, MA: MIT Press, 2013.

Juran, Nathan H., dir. *The 7th Voyage of Sinbad*. Columbia Pictures, 1958.

Juul, Jesper. *Half-Real: Video Games Between Real Rules and Fictional Worlds*. Cambridge, MA: MIT Press, 2005.

Kant, Immanuel. *Critique of Judgement*. Edited by Nicholas Walker. Translated by James Creed Meredith. Oxford World's Classics. Oxford: Oxford University Press, 2007.

Kearney, Richard. *Strangers, Gods, and Monsters: Interpreting Otherness*. London: Routledge, 2003.

Keogh, Brendan, and Darshana Jayemanne. "'Game Over, Man. Game Over': Looking at the Alien in Film and Videogames." *Arts* 7, no. 3 (August 2018): 43. https://doi.org/10.3390/arts7030043.

Kerr, Aphra. *Global Games: Production, Circulation and Policy in the Networked Era*. London: Routledge/Taylor & Francis Group, 2017.

Kikizo Staff. "Shadow of the Colossus: Exclusive New Interview, All-New Trailer & Screens." *Kikizo Archives*, March 21, 2005. http://archive.videogamesdaily.com/features/shadowofthecolossus_interview_march05.asp.

Kleivan, Inge, and Birgitte Sonne. *Eskimos—Greenland and Canada*. Iconography of Religions, Arctic Peoples, Volume: 2. Leiden, Netherlands: E. J. Brill, 1985.

Kneale, James. "From beyond: H. P. Lovecraft and the Place of Horror." *Cultural Geographies* 13, no. 1 (January 2006): 106–126. https://doi.org/10.1191/1474474005eu353oa.

Kocurek, Carly A. "Who Hearkens to the Monster's Scream? Death, Violence and the Veil of the Monstrous in Video Games." *Visual Studies* 30, no. 1 (January 2015): 79–89. https://doi.org/10.1080/1472586X.2015.996402.

Konami. *Metal Gear Solid*. Sony PlayStation. Konami, 1998.

Kress, Gunther, and Theo Van Leeuwen. *Reading Images: The Grammar by Visual Design*. London: Routledge, 1996.

Kristeva, Julia. *Powers of Horror: An Essay on Abjection*. European Perspectives. New York: Columbia University Press, 1982.

Krzywinska, Tanya. "The Gamification of Gothic Coordinates in Videogames." *Revenant* 1, no. 1 (2015): 58–78.

———. "Gaming Horror's Horror: Representation, Regulation, and Affect in Survival Horror Videogames." *Journal of Visual Culture* 14, no. 3 (December 2015): 293–297. https://doi.org/10.1177/14704129 15607924.

———. "Gothic American Gaming." In *The Cambridge Companion to American Gothic*, edited by Jeffrey Andrew Weinstock, 229–242. Cambridge: Cambridge University Press, 2017.

———. "Zombies in Gamespace: Form, Context, and Meaning in Zombie-Based Video Games." In *Zombie Culture: Autopsies of the Living Dead*, edited by Shawn McIntosh and Marc Leverette, 153–168. Lanham, MD: Scarecrow Press, 2008.

Kuchera, Ben. "*Shadow of Mordor*'s Nemesis System Is Simpler than You Think, and Should Be Stolen." *Polygon*, October 13, 2014. https://www.polygon.com/2014/10/13/6970533/shadow-of-mordors-nemesis -system-is-simpler-than-you-think-and-should.

Kuntz, Robert, and James Ward. *Gods, Demi-Gods & Deities*. Dungeons & Dragons, Supplement IV. Lake Geneva, WI: TSR Games, 1976.

Kushner, David. *Masters of Doom: How Two Guys Created an Empire and Transformed Pop Culture*. New York: Random House, 2004.

Lacina, Dia. "Monster Hunter World Can't Envision That Maybe Hunters Are the Baddies." *Paste Magazine*, February 28, 2019. https://www.pastemagazine.com/games/monster-hunter-world/monster -hunter-world-cant-envision-that-maybe-hunt/.

LaLone, Nicolas. "A Tale of Dungeons & Dragons and the Origins of the Game Platform." *Analog Game Studies* 6, no. 3 (September 2019). https://analoggamestudies.org/2019/09/a-tale-of-dungeons-dragons -and-the-origins-of-the-game-platform/.

Lamoureux, Mark. "8-Bit Primitive: Homage to the Atari 2600." In *Gamers: Writers, Artists & Programmers on the Pleasure of Pixels*, edited by Shana Compton, 78–91. New York: Soft Skull Press, 2004.

Latour, Bruno. *Reset Modernity!: The Field Book*. Edited by Bruno Latour, Martin Guinard-Terrin, Christophe Leclerq, Caroline Jansky, and Ulrike Havemann. Karlsruhe: ZKM Center for Art and Media, 2016.

Leesberg, Marjolein. "The Royal Game of Cupid: A 17th-Century Board Game." British Library: Picturing Places. Accessed August 21, 2021. https://www.bl.uk/picturing-places/articles/the-royal-game-of -cupid-a-17th-century-board-game.

Levidow, Les, and Kevin Robins, eds. *Cyborg Worlds: The Military Information Society*. London: Free Association Books, 1989.

Liberman, Anatoly. "Bugs: An Etymological Postscript." *OUPblog*, June 3, 2015. https://blog.oup.com/2015/06/bug-etymology-word-origin/.

Lofgren, Eric T., and Nina H. Fefferman. "The Untapped Potential of Virtual Game Worlds to Shed Light on Real World Epidemics." *The Lancet Infectious Diseases* 7, no. 9 (September 2007): 625–629. https://doi.org/10.1016/S1473-3099(07)70212-8.

Lord British. *Akalabeth*. Apple II. California Pacific Computer Company, 1980.

Lovecraft, Howard Phillips. *Supernatural Horror in Literature*. Mineola, NY: Dover Publications, 1973.

———. *Tales of H. P. Lovecraft*. Edited by Joyce Carol Oates. New York: HarperPerennial, 2007.

Luckhurst, Roger. "After Monster Theory?: Gareth Edwards's *Monsters*." *Science Fiction Film & Television* 13, no. 2 (July 2020): 269–290. https://doi.org/10.3828/sfftv.2020.14.

———. *Zombies: A Cultural History*. London: Reaktion Books, 2015.

MacCallum-Stewart, Esther, Jaakko Stenros, and Staffan Björk. "The Impact of Role-Playing Games on Culture." In *Role-Playing Game Studies: Transmedia Foundations*, edited by José P. Zagal and Sebastian Deterding, 172–187. New York: Routledge, 2018.

MacCormack, Patricia. "Posthuman Teratology." In *The Ashgate Research Companion to Monsters and the Monstrous*, edited by Asa Simon Mittman and Peter Dendle, 293–310. Ashgate Research Companions. Farnham, UK: Ashgate, 2013.

Maher, Jimmy. "A Word on Akalabeth and Chronology." *The Digital Antiquarian* (blog), December 2, 2011. https://www.filfre.net/2011/12/a-word-on-akalabeth-and-chronology/.

———. "Akalabeth." *The Digital Antiquarian* (blog), December 18, 2011. https://www.filfre.net/2011/12/akalabeth/.

Malchow, H. L. "Frankenstein's Monster and Images of Race in Nineteenth-Century Britain." *Past & Present* 139, no. 1 (May 1993): 90–130. https://doi.org/10.1093/past/139.1.90.

Maloy, Deirdre L. "The Swordthrust Series: A Survey." *Computer Gaming World* 2, no. 1 (January 1982): 12.

Mayfair Games. *Monsters of Myth & Legend*. Role Aids. Chicago: Mayfair Games, 1984.

Mäyrä, Frans. *Demonic Texts and Textual Demons: The Demonic Tradition, the Self, and Popular Fiction*. Tampere Studies in Literature and Textuality. Tampere, Finland: Tampere University Press, 1999.

———. "From the Demonic Tradition to Art-Evil in Digital Games: Monstrous Pleasures in *Lord of the Rings Online*." In *Ringbearers: The Lord of the Rings Online as Intertextual Narrative*, edited by Tanya Krzywinska, Esther MacCallum-Stewart, and Justin Parsler, 111–135. Manchester: Manchester University Press, 2011.

McCormack, Jon, and Alan Dorin. "Art, Emergence and the Computational Sublime." In *Proceedings of Second Iteration: A Conference on Generative Systems in the Electronic Arts*, 67–81. Melbourne: CEMA, 2001.

McGregor, Georgia Leigh. "Situations of Play: Patterns of Spatial Use in Videogames." In *Situated Play, Proceedings of DiGRA 2007 Conference*. Digital Games Research Association, 2007. http://www.digra.org /wp-content/uploads/digital-library/07312.05363.pdf.

McWhertor, Michael. "Bloodborne Review: Scarlett Letter." *Polygon*, March 27, 2015. https://www.polygon.com/2015/3/27/8209199 /bloodborne-review-PS4-playstation-4-exclusive.

———. "Hidetaka Miyazaki on Dark Souls 3's Changes to Bosses, Magic, Combat and More." *Polygon*, August 10, 2015. https://www .polygon.com/2015/8/10/9115299/dark-souls-3-hidetaka-miyazaki -interview-gamescom.

Mearls, Mike, ed. *Dungeons & Dragons: Volo's Guide to Monsters*. Renton, WA: Wizards of the Coast, 2016.

Mechner, Jordan. *Prince of Persia*. Apple II. Brøderbund Software, 1989.

———. *The Making of Prince of Persia: Journals, 1985–1993*. South San Francisco: Stripe Press, 2020.

Midway. *Invaders from the Outer Space (The Invaders)*. Arcade. Midway, 1970.

———. *Monster Gun*. Arcade. Midway, 1967.

Mittman, Asa Simon. *Maps and Monsters in Medieval England*. Studies in Medieval History and Culture. New York: Routledge, 2006.

Monnens, Devin, and Martin Goldberg. "Space Odyssey: The Long Journey of *Spacewar!* from MIT to Computer Labs Around the World." In "Cultural History of Video Games." Special issue, *Kinephanos* 5 (June 2015): 124–147.

Monolith Productions. *Middle-Earth: Shadow of Mordor*. PC. WB Games, 2014.

———. *Middle-Earth: Shadow of War*. PC. WB Games, 2017.

Mortensen, Torill Elvira, and Kristine Jørgensen. *The Paradox of Transgression in Games*. New York: Routledge, 2020.

Morteshka. *Black Book*. PC. HypeTrain Digital, 2021.

Mul, Jos de. "The (Bio)Technological Sublime." *Diogenes* 59, no. 1–2 (February 2012): 32–40. https://doi.org/10.1177/0392192112469162.

Muratova, Xenia. "Workshop Methods in English Late Twelfth-Century Illumination and the Production of Luxury Bestiaries." In *Beasts and Birds of the Middle Ages*, edited by Willene B. Clark and Meredith T. McMunn, 53–68. Philadelphia: University of Pennsylvania Press, 1989. https://doi.org/10.9783/9781512805512-005.

Murray, Janet H. *Hamlet on the Holodeck: The Future of Narrative in Cyberspace*. Cambridge, MA: MIT Press, 1998.

Murray, Wil, ed. *Bloodborne Collector's Edition Guide*. Hamburg: Future Press, 2015.

MUSE. "Mobile." MUDspeke Index. Updated September 23, 1999. https://mud.co.uk/muse/mobile.htm.

Nagel, Thomas. "What Is It Like to Be a Bat?" *The Philosophical Review* 83, no. 4 (October 1974): 435–450. https://doi.org/10.2307/2183914.

Namco. *Galaga*. Arcade. Namco, 1981.

———. *Xevious*. Arcade. Namco, 1982.

Naughty Dog. *The Last of Us*. PS3. Sony Computer Entertainment, 2013.

———. *The Last of Us Part II*. PS4. Sony Interactive Entertainment, 2020.

Nietzsche, Friedrich Wilhelm. *Beyond Good and Evil: Prelude to a Philosophy of the Future*. Edited by Rolf-Peter Horstmann and Judith Norman. Cambridge Texts in the History of Philosophy. Cambridge: Cambridge University Press, 2002.

Nintendo. *Super Mario Bros*. SNES. Nintendo, 1985.

———. *The Legend of Zelda*. Nintendo Entertainment System. Nintendo, 1987.

Ooijen, Erik van. "On the Brink of Virtual Extinction: Hunting and Killing Animals in Open World Video Games." *Eludamos. Journal for Computer Game Culture* 9, no. 1 (September 2018): 33–45.

Origin Systems. *Ultima VI: The False Prophet.* PC. Origin Systems, 1990.

O'Sullivan, James. "Collective Consciousness in Science Fiction." *Foundation* 39, no. 110 (Winter 2010): 80–85.

Papp, Zilia. *Anime and Its Roots in Early Japanese Monster Art.* Folkestone, UK: Global Oriental, 2010.

Pellett, Dirk. "Open Letter to ClassicGaming.Com." Dirk Pellet's WWW Home Page. Updated April 28, 2006. http://www.armory.com/~dlp /dnd1.html.

Perron, Bernard, ed. "Introduction: Gaming After Dark." In *Horror Video Games: Essays on the Fusion of Fear and Play*, 3–13. Jefferson, NC: McFarland & Co, 2009.

———. *The World of Scary Video Games: A Study in Videoludic Horror.* New York: Bloomsbury Academic, 2018.

Petersen, Sandy. *Call of Cthulhu.* Oakland: Chaosium, 1981.

Peterson, Jon. *Playing at the World: A History of Simulating Wars, People and Fantastic Adventures, from Chess to Role-Playing Games.* San Diego: Unreason Press, 2013.

———. *The Elusive Shift: How Role-Playing Games Forged Their Identity.* Game Histories. Cambridge, MA: MIT Press, 2020.

Peterson, Joseph H. *The Lesser Key of Solomon: Lemegeton Clavicula Salomonis.* York Beach, ME: Samuel Weiser, 2001.

Phobia Game Studio. *Carrion.* PC. Devolver Digital, 2020.

Pimper, Jeff, and Steve Perrin. *All the Worlds' Monsters.* Albany, CA: Chaosium, 1977.

Pinchbeck, Dan. "POCG2016 Dan Pinchbeck The Unreliable Philosophics of The Chinese Room." Philosophy of Computer Games Lectures, May 2, 2017. YouTube video, 1:04:14. https://www.youtube .com/watch?v=YqFjBWeNLRY.

Plater, Michael de, Christopher Herman Hoge, Robert Kenyon Hull Roberts, Daniel Paul Valerius, Rocky Albert Newton, and Kevin Leslie Stephens. Nemesis Characters, Nemesis Forts, Social Vendettas and Followers in Computer Games. US Patent US20160279522A1, filed March 25, 2016, and issued September 29, 2016. https://patents .google.com/patent/US20160279522A1/en.

Platinum Games. *Bayonetta.* PS3. Sega, 2009.

PlayStation. "*God of War*'s Bestiary: The Troll | Countdown to Launch." PlayStation, April 17, 2018. YouTube video, 1:43. https://www.youtube.com/watch?v=AVDWOiYXpv0.

Polinsky, Paige V. *Pokémon Designer: Satoshi Tajiri*. Toy Trailblazers. Minneapolis: Abdo Publishing, 2017.

Poots, Adam. *Kingdom Death: Monster*. Tabletop. Kingdom Death, 2015.

Purslow, Matt. "Developers, Why Aren't You Using the Nemesis System? Making a Case for the Generation's Best New Mechanic." *PCGamesN*, March 30, 2017. https://www.pcgamesn.com/middle-earth-shadow-of-war/shadow-of-mordor-nemesis-system-clones.

Rankin, Joy Lisi. *A People's History of Computing in the United States*. Cambridge, MA: Harvard University Press, 2018.

Rawitsch, Don, Bill Heinemann, and Paul Dillenberger. *The Oregon Trail*. HP 2100. 1971.

Rebellion Developments. *Aliens vs. Predator*. PC. Sega, 2010.

Reed, Kristan. "Interview of the Colossus." *Eurogamer*, November 10, 2005. https://www.eurogamer.net/articles/i_sotc_ps2.

Reeves, Matt, dir. *Cloverfield*. Paramount Pictures, 2008.

Rehak, Bob. "Materializing Monsters: Aurora Models, Garage Kits and the Object Practices of Horror Fandom." *The Journal of Fandom Studies* 1, no. 1 (November 2012): 27–45. https://doi.org/10.1386/jfs.1.1.27_1.

———. "Playing at Being: Psychoanalysis and the Avatar." In *The Video Game Theory Reader*, edited by Mark J. P. Wolf and Bernard Perron, 103–127. New York: Routledge, 2003.

Remedy Entertainment. *Control*. PC. 505 Games, 2019.

Retro Gamer. "Nishikado-San Speaks." *Retro Gamer* 1, no. 3 (2004): 35.

Riot Games. *League of Legends*. PC. Riot Games, 2009.

Rob. "Cross post from EQVault Board." Post on alt.games.everquest Google Group. December 22, 1998. https://groups.google.com/g/alt.games.everquest/c/XIKjYc6LrqY/m/xVRlUbphjRQJ.

Robinson, Martin. *The Art of Dead Space*. London: Titan Books, 2013.

Romalis, Sheila. "The East Greenland Tupilaq Image: Old and New Visions." *Études/Inuit/Studies* 7, no. 1 (1983): 152–159.

Romero, John. "Cyberdemon model scan, circa 1993." Twitter, December 10, 2014. https://twitter.com/romero/status/542616760789127170.

Ruberg, Bonnie. "Straight-Washing 'Undertale': Video Games and the Limits of LGBTQ Representation." *Transformative Works and Cultures* 28 (September 2018). https://doi.org/10.3983/twc.2018.1516.

Samyn, Michaël. "Bayonetta and the Vatican." *Notgames Blog*, April 27, 2010. https://web.archive.org/web/20100610203419/http://notgames .org/blog/2010/04/27/bayonetta-and-the-vatican/.

Santa Monica Studio. "God of War." PlayStation.com. Accessed June 20, 2018. https://web.archive.org/web/20210616211244/https://godofwar .playstation.com/stories/deconstructing-hr%C3%A6zlyr.

———. *God of War*. PS4. Sony Interactive Entertainment, 2018.

———. "Making of—God of War (2005) [Behind the Scenes]." NeoGamer—The Video Game Archive, uploaded 2020. YouTube video, 13:24. https://www.youtube.com/watch?v=VHdbIyE3A24&ab _channel=NeoGamer-TheVideoGameArchive.

Schrank, Brian. *Avant-Garde Videogames: Playing with Technoculture*. Cambridge, MA: MIT Press, 2014.

Sconce, Jeffrey. *Haunted Media: Electronic Presence from Telegraphy to Television*. Console-Ing Passions. Durham, NC: Duke University Press, 2000.

Scott, Ridley, dir. *Alien*. 20th Century Fox, 1979.

Sega. *Invaders (SEGA Invaders)*. Arcade. Sega, 1972.

———. *Monster Gun*. Arcade. Sega, 1972.

Sega. *Golden Axe*. Arcade. Sega, 1989.

Shamoon, Evan, ed. *The Art of God of War*. Milwaukie, OR: Dark Horse Books, 2018.

Shapiro, Fred R. "Etymology of the Computer Bug: History and Folklore." *American Speech* 62, no. 4 (Winter 1987): 376–378. https://doi.org /10.2307/455415.

Shildrick, Margrit. *Embodying the Monster: Encounters with the Vulnerable Self*. Theory, Culture & Society. London: SAGE Publications, 2002.

———. "Visual Rhetorics and the Seductions of the Monstrous: Some Precautionary Observations." *Somatechnics* 8, no. 2 (September 2018): 163–177. https://doi.org/10.3366/soma.2018.0248.

Shinkle, Eugénie. "Videogames and the Digital Sublime." In *Digital Cultures and the Politics of Emotion: Feelings, Affect and Technological Change*, edited by Athina Karatzogianni and Adi Kuntsman,

94–108. London: Palgrave Macmillan UK, 2012. https://doi.org/10
.1057/9780230391345_6.

Sicart, Miguel. *The Ethics of Computer Games*. Cambridge, MA: MIT
Press, 2009.

Silicon Knights. *Eternal Darkness: Sanity's Requiem*. Nintendo Game-
Cube. Nintendo, 2002.

Silverlock. "Again where did you . . ." Comment on rec.games
.computer.ultima.online Google Group post "Raph has it wrong . . .
The Mage tower is not PK friendly!!!" December 4, 1998. https://
groups.google.com/g/rec.games.computer.ultima.online/c/QVd8iPtxs
-M/m/ew-Pu497eyMJ.

Sliva, Marty. "Top 100 Unforgettable Video Game Moments." IGN.
Accessed July 19, 2021. https://www.ign.com/lists/top-100-video
-game-moments.

smartalic5. "Amnesia Water Monster 360 [Lurker]." August 8, 2011. You-
Tube video, 0:56. https://www.youtube.com/watch?v=32Jbvw-Fm0U.

Smith, Alexander. *They Create Worlds: The Story of the People and Companies That Shaped the Video Game Industry*. Boca Raton, FL: CRC Press,
2020.

Smith, Matthew. *Manic Miner*. ZX Spectrum. Software Projects, 1983.

Snider, Tim. *Weird Works: Tome of Creatures Offbeat and Downright
Strange*. Mansfield, OH: TWS Hobbies, 1983.

Soderman, Braxton. *Against Flow: Video Games and the Flowing Subject*.
Cambridge, MA: MIT Press, 2021.

Sotamaa, Olli, and Jan Švelch, eds. *Game Production Studies*. Amsterdam: Amsterdam University Press, 2021. https://doi.org/10.5117
/9789463725439.

Squire, Michael. "'Fantasies so Varied and Bizarre': The Domus Aurea,
the Renaissance, and the 'Grotesque.'" In *A Companion to the Neronian
Age*, edited by Emma Buckley and Martin T. Dinter, 444–464. Oxford:
Wiley-Blackwell, 2013. https://doi.org/10.1002/9781118316771.ch25.

St. Andre, Ken. *Tunnels & Trolls*. 1975. 1st ed. reprint, Phoenix: Flying
Buffalo, 2013.

Stainless Games. *Carmaggedon*. PC. Sales Curve Interactive, 1997.

Stang, Sarah. "Big Daddies and Their Little Sisters: Postfeminist Fatherhood in the Bioshock Series." In *Beyond the Sea: Navigating BioShock*,

edited by Felan Parker and Jessica Aldred, 27–49. Montreal: McGill-Queen's University Press, 2018.

———. "Shrieking, Biting, and Licking: The Monstrous-Feminine and Abject Female Monsters in Video Games." *Press Start* 4, no. 2 (January 2018): 18–34.

———. "The Broodmother as Monstrous-Feminine—Abject Maternity in Video Games." *Nordlit*, no. 42 (November 2019) 233–256. https://doi.org/10.7557/13.5014.

Stang, Sarah, and Aaron Trammell. "The Ludic Bestiary: Misogynistic Tropes of Female Monstrosity in *Dungeons & Dragons*." *Games and Culture* 15, no. 6 (2020): 730–747. https://doi.org/10.1177/1555412019850059.

Strassberg, Richard E., ed. *A Chinese Bestiary: Strange Creatures from the Guideways through Mountains and Seas*. Berkeley: University of California Press, 2002.

Strickland, Debra Higgs. "Monstrosity and Race in the Late Middle Ages." In *The Ashgate Research Companion to Monsters and the Monstrous*, edited by Asa Simon Mittman and Peter Dendle, 365–386. Farnham, UK: Ashgate, 2013. https://doi.org/10.4324/9781315241197.ch17.

Švelch, Jan. "Paratextuality in Game Studies: A Theoretical Review and Citation Analysis." *Game Studies* 20, no. 2 (June 2020). http://gamestudies.org/2002/articles/jan_svelch.

Švelch, Jaroslav. "Always Already Monsters—'*BioShock*''s (2007) 'Splicers' as Computational Others." *Nordlit*, no. 42 (November 2019). https://doi.org/10.7557/13.5015.

———. "Monsters by the Numbers: Controlling Monstrosity in Video Games." In *Monster Culture in the 21st Century: A Reader*, edited by Marina Levina and Diem-My T Bui, 193–208. New York: Bloomsbury Academic, 2013.

———. "Should the Monster Play Fair?: Reception of Artificial Intelligence in Alien: Isolation." *Game Studies* 20, no. 2 (June 2020). http://gamestudies.org/2002/articles/jaroslav_svelch.

———. "The Good, the Bad, and the Player: The Challenges to Moral Engagement in Single-Player Avatar-Based Video Games." In *Ethics and Game Design: Teaching Values through Play*, edited by Karen Schrier and David Gibson, 52–68. Hershey, PA: Information Science Reference, 2010.

Sychov Brothers. "Skeleton Lightweight." Unreal Engine [Marketplace], November 6, 2019. https://www.unrealengine.com/marketplace/en-US/product/skeleton-lightweight/reviews.

Taito. *Space Invaders*. Arcade. Taito, 1978.

Tally, Robert T. "Demonizing the Enemy, Literally: Tolkien, Orcs, and the Sense of the World Wars." *Humanities* 8, no. 1 (March 2019): 54. https://doi.org/10.3390/h8010054.

Tampere University Game Research Lab. "Monstrosity—The 17th Annual Tampere University Game Research Lab Spring Seminar." Tampere University of Applied Sciences. https://www.tuni.fi/en/news /monstrosity-17th-annual-tampere-university-game-research-lab-spring -seminar.

Taylor, Jay. "Interview Extra: Fumito Ueda (Ico, Shadow of the Colossus, The Last Guardian)." *Cane and Rinse*, August 27, 2019. https:// caneandrinse.com/fumito-ueda-interview/.

Taylor, Laurie N. "Not of Woman Born: Monstrous Interfaces and Monstrosity in Video Games." PhD diss., University of Florida, 2006. https:// ufdc.ufl.edu/UFE0013427/00001.

Taylor, T. L. *Play Between Worlds: Exploring Online Game Culture*. Cambridge, MA: MIT Press, 2009.

Team Ico. *Shadow of the Colossus*. PS2. Sony Computer Entertainment, 2005.

Team Salvato. *Doki Doki Literature Club*. PC. Team Salvato, 2017.

Thacker, Eugene. *Tentacles Longer than Night*. Horror of Philosophy 3. Winchester, UK: Zer0 Books, 2015.

The Coalition. *Gears 5*. PC. Xbox Game Studios, 2019.

The Indie Stone. *Project Zomboid [Early Access Version]*. PC. The Indie Stone, 2013.

Therrien, Carl. "Games of Fear: A Multi-Faceted Historical Account of the Horror Genre in Video Games." In *Horror Video Games: Essays on the Fusion of Fear and Play*, edited by Bernard Perron, 26–45. Jefferson, NC: McFarland & Co, 2009.

Thier, Dave. "Yes, AAA Single-Player Games Are Dying, And That's Fine." *Forbes*, October 18, 2017. https://www.forbes.com/sites/davidthier/2017 /10/18/star-wars-visceral-yes-aaa-single-player-games-are-dying-thats -fine/.

Thompson, Clive. "Who's the Boss?" *Wired*, May 8, 2006. https://web .archive.org/web/20080508192019/http:/www.wired.com/gaming /gamingreviews/commentary/games/2006/05/70832.

Thompson, Tommy. "The Perfect Organism." *Becoming Human*, April 24, 2017. https://becominghuman.ai/the-perfect-organism-d350c05d8960.

Tolkien, J. R. R. "Beowulf: The Monsters and the Critics." In *The Monsters and the Critics and Other Essays*, edited by Christopher Tolkien, 5–48. London: HarperCollins, 1997.

Topsfield, Andrew. "The Indian Game of Snakes and Ladders." *Artibus Asiae* 46, no. 3 (1985): 203–226. https://doi.org/10.2307/3250203.

TPN. *Phoenix*. Arcade. Taito, 1980.

Trammell, Aaron. "How *Dungeons & Dragons* Appropriated the Orient." *Analog Game Studies* 3, no. 1 (January 2016). http://analoggamestudies .org/2016/01/how-dungeons-dragons-appropriated-the-orient/.

Tucker, Richard, and Valerie Tucker. *Step Right up! Classic American Target and Arcade Forms*. Atglen, PA: Schiffer Publishing Ltd, 2014.

Turnbull, Don, ed. *Advanced Dungeons & Dragons: Fiend Folio*. Lake Geneva, WI: TSR Games, 1981.

Turnock, Julie A. *Plastic Reality: Special Effects, Technology, and the Emergence of 1970s Blockbuster Aesthetics*. Film and Culture. New York: Columbia University Press, 2015.

Tyler, Melissa. *Dark Age of Camelot: Prima's Official Strategy Guide*. Rev. ed. Roseville, CA: Prima Games, 2002.

Ubi Soft. *Rayman*. PC. Ubi Soft, 1995.

Ubisoft Montpellier. *ZombiU*. Wii U. Ubisoft, 2012.

Vance, Jack. *The Eyes of the Overworld*. New York: Ace Books, 1966.

Vella, Daniel. "No Mastery Without Mystery: Dark Souls and the Ludic Sublime." *Game Studies* 15, no. 1 (July 2015). http://gamestudies .org/1501/articles/vella.

Vinci, Leonardo da. *Notebooks*. Edited by Irma A. Richter and Thereza Wells. Oxford World's Classics. Oxford: Oxford University Press, 2008.

Visceral Games. *Dante's Inferno*. PS3. Electronic Arts, 2010.

Vitruvius Pollio, Marcus. *Vitruvius: Ten Books on Architecture*. Translated by Ingrid D. Rowland. New York: Cambridge University Press, 1999.

Wade, Alex. *The Pac-Man Principle: A User's Guide to Capitalism*. Winchester, UK: Zer0 Books, 2018.

Wark, McKenzie. *Gamer Theory*. Cambridge, MA: Harvard University Press, 2007.

Waterhouse, Ruth. "Beowulf as Palimpsest." In *Monster Theory: Reading Culture*, edited by Jeffrey Jerome Cohen, 26–39. Minneapolis: University of Minnesota Press, 1996.

Webley, Stephen J., and Peter Zackariasson, eds. *The Playful Undead and Video Games: Critical Analyses of Zombies and Gameplay*. Routledge Advances in Game Studies. New York: Routledge, 2020.

Webster, Andrew. "How New Technology Helped Make Monster Hunter World's Beasts Even More Terrifying." *Verge*, February 1, 2018. https://www.theverge.com/2018/2/1/16955336/monster-hunter-world-creature-design-interview.

Weinstock, Jeffrey Andrew. "Invisible Monsters: Vision, Horror, and Contemporary Culture." In *The Ashgate Research Companion to Monsters and the Monstrous*, edited by Asa Simon Mittman and Peter Dendle, 275–289. Ashgate Research Companions. Farnham, UK: Ashgate, 2013.

Weise, Matthew J. "How the Zombie Changed Videogames." In *Zombies Are Us: Essays on the Humanity of the Walking Dead*, edited by Christopher M. Moreman and Cory Rushton, 151–168. Jefferson, NC: McFarland, 2011.

———. "The Rules of Horror: Procedural Adaptation in Clock Tower, Resident Evil, and Dead Rising." In *Horror Video Games: Essays on the Fusion of Fear and Play*, edited by Bernard Perron, 238–266. Jefferson, NC: McFarland & Co, 2009.

Weiser, Jason. "Episode 2—And Only Rage Remained." *The Lost Pages of Norse Myth*, September 27, 2017. Podcast, 37:50. https://open.spotify.com/show/3fiW5OG2ry4NHGB0wmANVI.

———. "Episode 6—The Sundering of Jötunheim." *The Lost Pages of Norse Myth*, February 27, 2018. Podcast, 44:54. https://open.spotify.com/show/3fiW5OG2ry4NHGB0wmANVI.

Wengrow, David. "Gods and Monsters: Image and Cognition in Neolithic Societies." *Paléorient* 37, no. 1 (2011): 153–163.

———. *The Origins of Monsters: Image and Cognition in the First Age of Mechanical Reproduction*. The Rostovtzeff Lectures. Princeton: Princeton University Press, 2014.

Whisenhunt, Gary, Ray Wood, Dirk Pellett, and Flint Pellett. *dnd*. V. 5.4. PLATO. 1977.

White, Jeff. "Karl Guttag Conference on Delphi TI Net." Post on comp.sys.ti Google Group, February 11, 1993. https://groups.google.com/g/comp.sys.ti/c/QlLThkrm8Po/m/GtnkyhtF4nMJ.

Wilde, Tyler. "The Live Service Gold Rush Hasn't Stopped Single-player Games from Thriving." *PC Gamer*, March 18, 2021. https://www.pcgamer.com/singleplayer-games-live-service/.

Williams Electronics. *Defender*. Arcade. Williams Electronics, 1981.

Wiltshire, Alex. "How A Plague Tale: Innocence's Rat Hordes Were Made." *Rock Paper Shotgun*, December 18, 2019. https://www.rockpapershotgun.com/how-a-plague-tale-innocences-rat-hordes-were-made.

Wood, Andrew, and Adam Summerville. "Understanding Boss Battles: A Case Study of Cuphead." Paper presented at the *AIIDE Workshop on Experimental AI in Games 2019*. http://www.exag.org/archive/wood2019battles.pdf.

Yager Development. *Spec Ops: The Line*. PC. 2K Games, 2012.

Yannakakis, Georgios N., and Julian Togelius. *Artificial Intelligence and Games*. Cham, Switzerland: Springer International Publishing, 2018.

Yeh, Denny. "How Santa Monica Studio Created God of War's Greatest Challenge." *PlayStation.Blog*, February 1, 2019. https://blog.playstation.com/2019/02/01/how-santa-monica-studio-created-god-of-wars-greatest-challenge/.

Yin-Poole, Wesley. "Deus Ex Boss Battles Outsourced." *Eurogamer*, September 19, 2011. https://www.eurogamer.net/articles/2011-09-19-deus-ex-boss-battles-outsourced.

————. "Single-Player Games 'Gone in 3 Years.'" *Eurogamer*, August 16, 2011. https://www.eurogamer.net/articles/2011-08-16-single-player-only-games-gone-in-3-years.

Zeenoh. *Nightfall: Escape*. PC. Zeenoh Inc., 2016.

INDEX